Journey to Nubia and Kemet:
EXPLORING AFRICAN HISTORY, CULTURE AND CONTRIBUTIONS

Journey to Nubia and Kemet:
EXPLORING AFRICAN HISTORY, CULTURE AND CONTRIBUTIONS

Angel Brown-Harriott

2020

Copyright © 2015 by Angel D. Harriott

All rights reserved. This book or any portion thereof may not be reproduced or used in any manner whatsoever without the express written permission of the publisher except for the use of brief quotations in a book review or scholarly journal.

First Printing: 2015

ISBN: Print: 978-1-951881-04-7
ISBN: EBook: 978-1-951881-05-4
Cultured Melanin Literary & Visual Arts Studios
PO Box #4042
Baltimore, MD 21222
www.culturedmelanin.studio

Global Journey for Children, Inc.
www.globaljourneyforchildren.org
Phone: (301)910-7396

Dedication

To my family:

Thank you for your love and support

To children around the world, present and future:

Learn and appreciate the history and contributions of all people

Learn to value one another and appreciate the diversity of mankind

Learn to respect differences that enhance what we have to share and contribute

Learn to live and work together for the common good of all

Sya *(knowledge)*

Volume I

Journey to Nubia and Kemet

"Free and critical minds can emerge only by a return to the source –the primary source."…. Free and critical minds seek truth without chauvinism or shame."

- Dr. Asa Hilliard

"It is time for parents to teach young people early on that in diversity there is beauty and there is strength. We all should know that diversity makes for a rich tapestry, and we must understand that all the threads of the tapestry are equal in value no matter their color."

-Dr. Maya Angelou

Table of Contents

Dedication..1

Acknowledgements 5

Poem: TRANSITION 13 6

Introduction..7
   Author's Introduction..8
   Continent of Africa 15

Part One: History of Kemet (Egypt).. 16
   Chapter 1: An Introduction to Nile Valley Civilization.................................... 17
   Nile Valley & Nile River 18
   Kush (Nubia) 23
   Kemet (Egypt) 25
   Chapter 2: Agricultural Systems in Kemet... 32
   Chapter 3: Kemet's Government 35
   Kemetic Chronology: A Summary (Dr. Asa Hilliard, III) 37
   Review Questions 39

Part Two: Queens of Nile Valley Civilization... 40
   Chapter 4: Kushite Kingdoms 41
   Cities of Antiquity... 42
   Chapter 5: Kendakes from the Kingdom of Kush (Nubia) 46
   Origins of Kendakes: From Queens to Warriors... 47
   The Four Kendakes... 51
   Chapter 6: Queens of Kemet 55
   Nswt Nefertari 59
   Nswt Hatshepsut... 62
   Nswt Tiye... 66
   Review Questions 74

Part Three: Kings (Pharaohs) of Kemet 75
   Chapter 7: Pharaohs of High Culture 76
   Narmer... 78
   Taharqa 79
   Djoser... 80
   Ramesses II... 81
   Tuthmosis IV... 88
   Sarcophagus of King Tutankhamun 89
   Review Questions 92

Part Four: Imhotep 93
   Chapter 8: The World's First Multi-Genius 94
   Designer of the Step Pyramid.. 95
   Father of Medicine 98
   Review Questions 99

Part Five: Architectural Masterpieces of Kemet 100
Chapter 9: Magnificent Structures Built in Nubia and Kemet 101
Pyramids, Tekhen (Obelisks) and Temples 102
Excavating Kemet's Structures in Modern Times 106
Review Questions 110

Part Six: Kemet's Educational System 111
Chapter 10: Educating a Nation of People in Ancient Times 112
Origins of Kemet's Educational Systems 113
Sacred Language and Script 120
Numbers in Mdw Ntr (Hieroglyphics) 124

Part Seven: Kemetic Symbolism and Metaphors 125
Chapter 12: Signs of the Time in Kemet 126
Ankh 127
MA'AT 128
Eye of Heru (Horus) 129
Scarab Beetle 130
Review Questions 131

Summary 132

Glossary 133

Bibliography 137

Acknowledgements

The information and photographs contained in this book were compiled, condensed and edited from several sources.

I have great appreciation and respect for all of the Grand Master Teachers, or Kemetologists (*Term coined by Asa Hilliard, a historian who was dedicated to the study of Egypt during the time period in which Nile Valley Civilization existed and was called Kemet [1st – 25th Dynasties]*), Egyptologists, archaeologists, anthropologists and other historians who have dedicated their professional lives to unearthing and sharing the true history of Africa and people of African ancestry. Thank you for providing the information, documentation, and artifacts that validate the existence, contributions and journey of Africans. While there continues to be many individuals who unveil, document and digitize African history, there are a few who have contributed directly to my education and ability to create a venue for children to capture this history.

A special thanks to:

Dr. Marimba Ani	Dr. John Henrik Clarke
Anthony T. Browder	Dr. Asa Hilliard
Joseph Campbell	Dr. Yosef A.A. ben-Jochannan
Dr. Frances Cress Welsing	Clyde McElvene
Cheikh Anta Diop	Dr. Ivan Van Sertima
Dr. Charles S. Finch, III	Dr. George G.M. James
Cedric Harriott	Dr. Chancellor Williams

I would like to express my appreciation and special acknowledgement to Anthony Browder for reviewing my original manuscript, sharing additions to this book and for all the work he has done to enlighten us about African history for 30 years.

I would like to extend a special acknowledgement to my content editor, Clyde McElvene, who spent considerable time researching and vetting the content and materials in the book as well as sharing his personal insights and experiences with respect to African history.

Poem: TRANSITION 13

We knew not
We studied
We learned all there was to know
We taught others

Then we forgot what we had learned
And then forgot that we had forgotten

Now we are taught
(By those who were once taught by us)
Knowledge
(That we already had)

So...
We study
We learn all there is to know
We teach others

Will we forget....AGAIN?

Anthony T. Browder
- *Cultural Historian*

Introduction

Who are you?

Where did you come from?

How did you get here?

"When "AFRICAN SCHOLARS" interpret their own African history from an African perspective, for an African reading public everywhere, including the United States of America, then, and only then, shall we have TRUE AFRICAN HISTORY."

– Dr. Yosef A.A. ben-Jochannan

Author's Introduction

"If a race has no history, if it has no worthwhile tradition, it becomes a negligible factor in the thought of the world and it stands in danger of being exterminated." - *Carter G. Woodson*

This book is the first in a series for my ancestors, family and communities of people around the globe. The theme of the series is **Sankofa:** going back to move forward; reconnecting, and rebuilding relationships with who we are. It is a resource that can be used as a part of an inclusive curriculum (lesson plan), developed with consideration for everyone's historical and cultural identity and contributions to society. The book should be used to teach children in history and social studies courses in the United States of America's school systems and other countries about African history.

Many of us have heard stories about African people who were kidnapped from their homeland as a result of the European slave-trade and forced to come to the United States of America (USA) and other countries. What many people do not know is the true story of these kidnapped Africans **before** they were forcefully taken from their homeland. Who were they? How did they live? Where did they come from in Africa? Some African and non-African people may not have any idea of what effect being forcefully removed from their homeland had on the ability of African people to see themselves as connected to other Africans all over the world. What have you been told about this time in history? What do you know about the culture, history and contributions of Africans?

This book, from this point on, will refer to the European slave-trade as the "MAAFA". This Swahili term was adopted by Dr. Marimba Ani, an anthropologist and scholar who studied African culture. She used this term to describe the disaster, damage, injustice, and suffering of Africans during the slave-trade and beyond. Although there are many books that include the history of Africans while they were held in captivity in America, very few books used in our history or social studies courses explain the culture and life of Africans while they lived in their native continent of Africa before the MAAFA. Therefore, many children have been and are still being taught that the lives, history and culture of Africans started with African captivity, or slavery. This is not true. The truth is that the story of Africans started hundreds, even thousands

years before Europeans ever sailed to the shores of Africa or America. In fact, Africa's story started long before the organized nations of America, Greece or Rome existed.

As we know from scientists who have studied the origins of mankind, the first human beings on earth came from Africa. Therefore, the Africans brought to America against their will more than 250 years ago were at least the great, great, great, great, great, great grandchildren of the **mothers and fathers of civilization.** That's a lot of greats!

The African proverb says, "Until the lion has his own storyteller the hunter will always have the best stories." It is the stories of those ancestors that must be continually told by *their* children. We must begin to educate children about this history from the beginning.

There is some evidence of Africa's contributions to civilization throughout Washington, DC, such as The Blashfield Mural located in the Library of Congress, the Washington Monument and, more recently, the National Museum of African American History and Culture which highlights great contributions of African Americans. However, Kemet's (the original name for ancient Egypt) influence on Washington, DC's architecture, such as the Lincoln Memorial, and in the layout and design of many structures that may be found throughout the nation's Capital, are direct connections to the contributions of Africans and the continent of Africa before their presence in America. You can see an example of this influence when you look at the illustrations on the following pages which shows the Washington Monument in Washington, DC and the monument of Queen Hatshepsut and King Thutmose I located at the Karnak Temple in Kemet (ancient Egypt) along the Nile River. In this book, we will explore those connections, properly identify these symbols and show why these symbols and structures, along with many others, are attributed to Africa, specifically early Nile Valley civilization.

It is exemplary and expected that African-centered schools include this history and culture in their curriculum but most children in the United States will not attend an African-centered school. Yet, to foster an attitude of **global citizenship** it is important for all children to be formally taught about the contributions made by Africans who lived in America during their 250 plus years of captivity and after. It is not enough to briefly explore the history of African Americans during Black

history month. You might wonder why it is important for children to know this history. Well, it is important for children to know because no people have contributed to and sacrificed more toward the construction and civilization of the USA and many other countries than Black Africans. When they arrived in America, they brought with them their skills and knowledge from all over the continent of Africa. Yet, people of African ancestry around the world are too often thought of as inferior to others since a complete and accurate account of African history and contributions are not currently included in many schools' curriculum.

The illustration above reflects detail of Blashfield's mural in dome collar showing America's contribution of science and Egypt's (Kemet's) contribution of written records in the Library of Congress. (Located in Washington, DC). The mural starts with Egypt, which introduced writing along with a portrait of the first recorded Egyptian King, Mena. The mural ends with America as represented by Abraham Lincoln, the 16th President of the USA.

Luxor Temple, East Bank of the Nile River

Washington Monument, Washington, DC
By Diliff - Own work, CC BY-SA 2.5,

An important goal of this series is to dispel the misconceptions that some children and adults have about Africa today, including the lack of Africa's contributions to the rest of the world. Dr. Francis Cress-Welsing, a well-known psychiatrist who practiced in Washington, DC said, "I won't rest until Black children are taught to love themselves as THEMSELVES". With this series, I strive to continue her efforts.

As you begin to develop ideas, thoughts, principles (rules or standards) and concepts necessary for a successful life it is important that you are given accurate information from which to form these ideas, concepts, principles and thoughts. You need to be able to answer three important questions: Who am I? Where in the world am I? How did I get here? Can you answer those questions? If you cannot, you are not alone. Since I undertook the research for this book I have acquired a great amount of information; answers to questions about African history, culture and contributions that I did not know. For hundreds of years many people could not answer these questions because some people intentionally prevented them from acquiring knowledge about African history. There was a deliberate destruction of African culture and contributions and the records of that culture. For generations, some European scholars attempted to deny that Kemet (Egypt) was even a part of Africa. However, we know through the research and findings of historians, anthropologists and archaeologists, that not only was Kemet a part of Africa but the Nile Valley was the world's first cultural highway made up of a blend of many African cultures.

The remains of Kemet (Ancient Egypt) can be compared to a crime scene that has gone unsolved for years, affected by the weather and witnesses who have passed away. Since moving objects around can ruin clues as to what happened, when police investigators arrive at a crime scene, they prefer that everything remain as it was when the crime was committed. They need as many clues as possible to find out what happened. Just as detectives need evidence to solve a crime, researchers, historians, archaeologists, geologists, anthropologists, Kemetologists and other scientists need evidence to prove what happened in the past. Investigating prehistory is similar to investigating a *crime scene* that takes place on a much larger scale. The more evidence there is, the greater the possibility that researchers can determine what happened, when it occurred, and who was involved. In the case of Kemet, much of the evidence still exist leaving us with undisputable facts necessary to determine what really happened and when.

Sometimes, physical evidence and historical facts are influenced by assumptions that individuals have when they evaluate evidence. For example, researchers who believe civilization has only recently accomplished a high level of technical achievement will tend to ignore any evidence that suggest a different result no matter how strong the evidence may be. One way to respond to this bias (prejudice) is to consider expert analysis from other disciplines. So, in this series I will **introduce expert analysis** from astronomy, engineering, geology, and anthropology, as well as insights from noted historians. As I discuss the origins of Kemetian (Egyptian) civilization I will explore artifacts, which include everything from skeletal remains to stone vases, jewelry temples, and other monuments, that are considered primary pieces of evidence. Among these are the pyramids of Kemet (Egypt), especially the Great Pyramid, which is one of the largest and oldest monuments. The pyramid was named "Her-em-akhet" which means "Heru on the horizon". The Greeks called it a "Sphinx". These monuments have been dated to approximately 5,000 B.C.E. (Before the Common Era) and before Rome, Greece or America. These are structures we can see that provide facts that have been examined and scientifically tested and verified by researchers. When you

examine all of the information compiled by these researchers, it provides a more complete picture of Kemet's (Egypt's) pre-history, as you will discover in this book.

Racism is a tragedy that has played a big part in shaping world history and telling stories about Africans, and other ethnicities, which negatively influences all people. We must remember that there is only one race, "the human race" which has been proven to have originated in Africa, the birthplace of man and civilization. So, this book is for everybody. Because of how Africans were brought to America, African history and American history are intertwined and can never be separated. Therefore, we have a responsibility to teach *all* children about both – African history and African-American history. Children of African ancestry, in particular, must be taught their true story, and have knowledge of what their ancestors accomplished and contributed to the ancient world and modern society. To do this, they must be provided with information and stories that tells them who they are and where they came from.

Dr. John Henry Clarke says:

> *"History should tell a people who they are, where they came from and what their potential is as a people. If it fails to do so it is useless. The name that people call themselves must provide them with an understanding of their history by connecting them to a **landmass, a language, a culture, a religion and a philosophy.** If a people's name fails to accomplish these simple tasks, their name is useless."*

An African moved across the Atlantic Ocean against his or her will is still an African. To put it a different way, if French pastries are cooked and served in a Kentucky restaurant it doesn't make them Kentucky pastries. They are still French pastries. Likewise, an African moved across the Atlantic Ocean is still an African.

It has been said that the only thing new are those things which have been forgotten. We must let the circle be unbroken and share knowledge so we can continue to build upon the contributions of our ancestors and shine a light on some of the African history that has been forgotten. Let's get ready to travel back in time over 5,000 years ago to a land far away that Africans called "home".

Angel Brown-Harriott
Sya (knowledge)

Continent of Africa

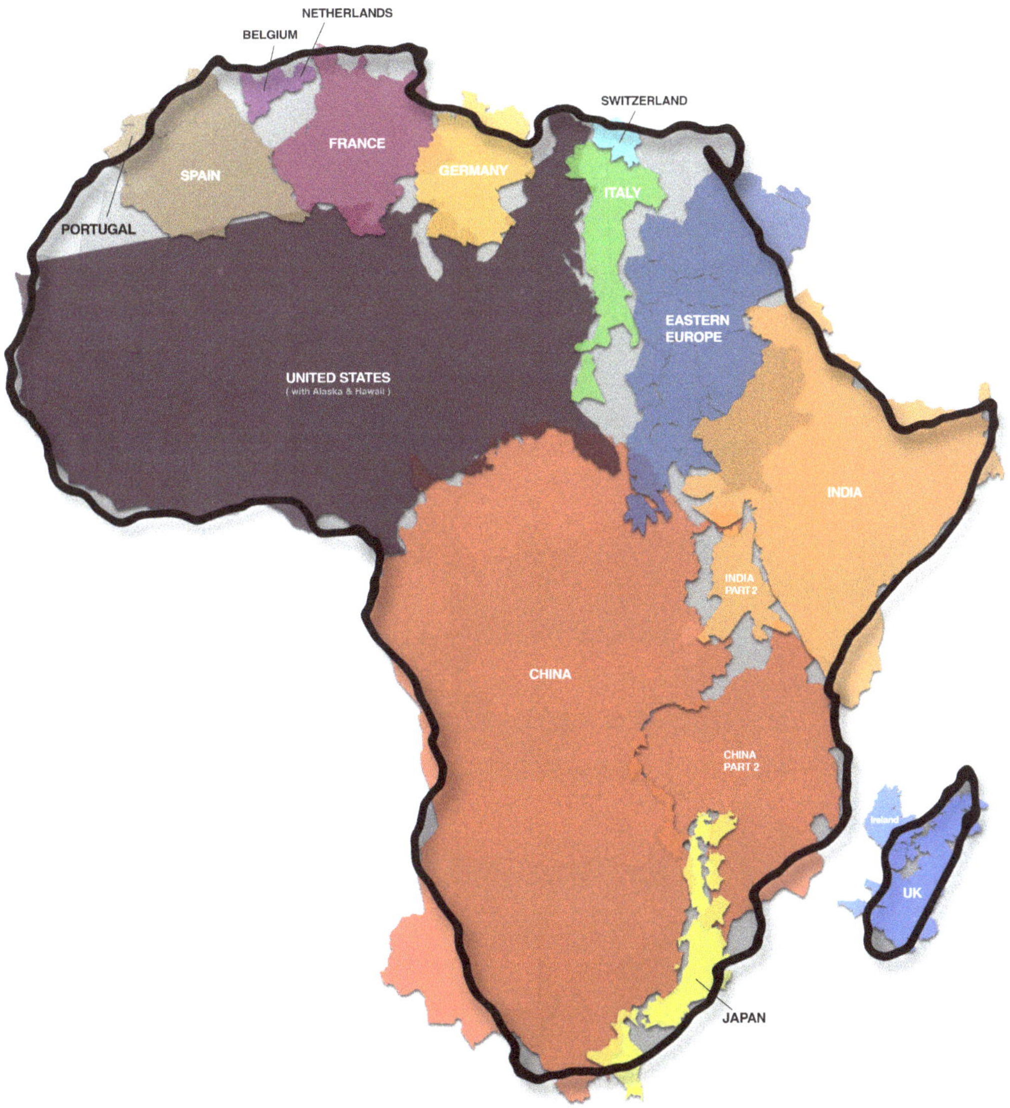

This map demonstrates how large the continent of Africa is compared to other countries and continents in the world. As you can see, the United States, China, India, Mexico, Eastern Europe, Italy, Germany and Spain all fit within the frame outlined in white that represents the continent of Africa. Most maps today erroneously show Africa in dimensions that are comparable in size to many of the countries shown above. The Peters Projection Map best represents true sizes. There are 54 recognized countries in the continent of Africa.

7 Continents in order by size:

Asia, Africa, North America, South America, Antarctica Europe, Australia

Part One

History of Kemet (Egypt)

Chapter 1: An Introduction to Nile Valley Civilization

You will discover:

- ❖ The location of the Nile Valley, Nubia & Kemet.
- ❖ How people lived and worked in Kemet and the significance of the Nile River and Nile Valley.
- ❖ Kemet's many contributions to the world.

Important words to know:

civilization	dynasty	papyrus	hieroglyphics
Kemet	sustain	irrigation	Medu Netcher
Kemite	Nsw	reed	flood plains
Kemtwu	Nswt	scroll	natural irrigation
Chem	erected	hominoids	canal irrigation
workforce	cultivate	agriculture	domesticate

Early Origins

There is controversy about the early origin of mankind, but according to archaeological finds, the oldest **hominoids**, or human beings, in the world lived in Africa. Fossil remains suggest they were there several million years before they ever appeared anywhere else on earth. In 2015, the Science journal published an article about an international team of

> The oldest recorded civilization to date is located in the heart of Africa.

paleoanthropologists who discovered the oldest human fossil dated to be 2.8 million years old. The team found the fossils in 2013 during an excavation in Ethiopia which is located in Eastern Africa at the tip of the Nile River.

Christopher Klein A&E Networks 2015

Close up view of the mandible just steps from where it was sighted by Chalachew Seyoum, an ASU graduate student from Ethiopia.

If you can imagine a strip of land so long that it extends over 4,000 miles throughout the continent of Africa, you will see the Nile Valley. The Nile River, which runs through Nile Valley, is the longest river in Africa and in the world. If you traveled from New York City to California, you would still need to travel another 1,000 miles to equal the distance of the Nile Valley.

These maps compare the distance between California and New York in the United States of America and the length of the Nile River in Africa.

People from all over Africa came to this part of the continent and settled there bringing a diverse set of habits, customs, ideas and cultures. It was out of this mix of African cultures that **Kemet** was formed. Kemet, which is commonly known as Egypt today, was a group of many African nations that relied upon the Nile River. The Nile River is often referred to as the world's first cultural highway.

The Origins of the Nile River

Two great rivers, the White Nile and the Blue Nile, come together to form the Nile River. The Nile River, which measures about 4,160 miles long, flows up from the South down to the North and into the Mediterranean Sea. During the development of Nile Valley civilization, there were people who had the job of writing and maintaining important information. These people were called **scribes**. The Papyrus of Hunefer was a document written by scribes. It provides the historical documentation which tells us that the beginning of the Nile River was called the White Nile and its waters flow through present day Uganda. The Blue Nile flowed from the highlands of present day Ethiopia. The White Nile and the Blue Nile join together in Khartoum, the capital of modern day Sudan. These two bodies of water come together to form one body of water that empties into the Mediterranean Sea.

Why is the Nile River so important?

The Nile River sustained the civilization of ancient Kemet (Egypt) from 3,100 to 332 B.C. Nearly 2,500 years ago, Herodotus, an ancient Greek researcher and historian, called Kemet "the gift of the Nile" after he visited the nation. Can you imagine why he might have given the Nile River such a name? One of the main reasons he called it the "gift of the Nile" was because the Nile River deposited some of the world's best mineral-rich sediment (agricultural soil) along its **flood plains**. People settled and lived near the river in huts when they first inhabited the area, but eventually moved to highlands further away from the water. The highlands were called Upper Kemet and the lowlands were called Lower Kemet. The flood plains that occurred in the lowlands resulted in rich black topsoil that guaranteed abundant crops. For thousands of years, Kemet has been a great producer of cereal crops, fruits and vegetables. Because of the rich fertile soil created by the Nile River and the skills brought to this region by the people who settled there, they were able to prosper for over 3,000 years.

Some significant scientific contributions include the creation of **canal irrigation** (also called artificial irrigation) developed at the end of the pre-dynastic period. Before that time, Kemetians relied on **natural irrigation**. Natural irrigation occurs when water flows without artificial interruptions. Nathan Anderson was an engineer with the US Army Corp of Engineers. He indicated that canal irrigation was necessary to aid in the increased need for agricultural production as the population grew. They were also credited with constructing dams over 4,600 years ago to store large volumes of water to protect against floods. Some other contributions include the development of agricultural tools, such as:

1. shaduf – hydraulic lift device used to raise water to higher elevations
2. baddala- low-lift device used to transfer water from one field to another
3. saqiya – a cattle (or oxen) driven device that lifted water over 20 feet
4. tambur – low-head hydraulic lift device. It was later named "Archimedes Screw".

Today, people still rely on the Nile River for crops and other by-products as well as to sustain their animals. However, this water resource faces many of the same challenges as other nations that are concerned about water resources throughout the world today. Scientists are concerned about the quality of water and our ability to maintain sufficient supply to support farmers and consumers who rely on it. Many countries learned from the agricultural systems originally developed in Kemet.

Papyrus of Hunefer, (CC BY-NC-SA 4.0)British Museum

Scribes wrote on papyrus to document important information and to demonstrate customs and traditions through the use of pictures or *Medu Netcher. These types of papyrus scrolls provide historians with a lot of information about the culture of people who lived in ancient Kemet. Hunefer was a scribe during the 19th Dynasty. He was the scribe for the Papyrus of Hunefer and the Papyrus of Ani.

*Some Kemetic words are spelled differently when they are interpreted today. This is largely because the hieroglyphic language did not use vowels. For example, Mdw Ntr is the Kemetic name for hieroglyphics but it is commonly referred to as Medu Neter or Medu Netcher (Budge) to assist with pronunciation of the word.

Kush (Nubia)

We now know that the oldest recorded nation in the world was located in Africa in the Nile Valley. There was a highly developed civilization that the Africans called Kush and the Greeks later called Nubia. Nubia was a very wealthy nation, in large part, due to its huge supply of natural resources. The Nubian people were Black as we can observe from many of their paintings which show how they saw themselves. (See the illustration on the next page).

> **Anthropologists have determined that Kush is older than Kemet.**

Historians have determined that Nubia is older than Kemet. One of the reasons we know that Nubia is older than Kemet is because Medu Netcher (**hieroglyphics**) writings may be found throughout Nubia and Medu Netcher existed long before the first dynasty was established in Kemet. The hieroglyphics left behind has been critical to our knowledge and understanding of their culture and history. Another reason historians acknowledge that Nubia (Kingdom of Kush) existed before Kemet (Ancient Egypt) was because archaeologists found a burial ground with many tombs in Nubia. These tombs contained artifacts, such as jewelry and pottery, that confirmed the existence of the Nubian Kingdom and the fact that it preceded Kemet. Some historians believe that the people of Nubia actually migrated from Nubia to the northern region and called the new area where they settled Kemet. Nubia also supported Kemet when they were under attack by foreign invaders.

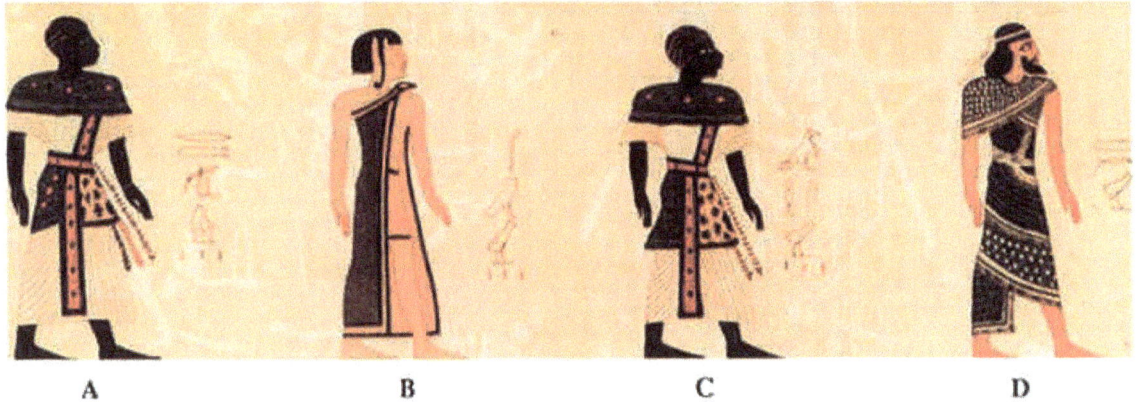

This painting from the tomb of Ramses 111 (1200 BC) shows that the Egyptians saw themselves as Blacks, and painted themselves as such without possible confusion with the Indo-Europeans [Caucasoids] or the Semites. It is a representation of the races in their most minute differences, which insures the accuracy of the colors. Throughout their entire history, the Egyptians never entertained the fantasy of portraying themselves by types B or D.

A) The Egyptian seen by himself, black type
B) The "Indo-European"
C) The other Blacks in Africa
D) The Semite

Photos by Sya - JNK, CC, British Museum

The stelas above illustrate how Nubian and Kemetian people drew and saw themselves. The text written on the bottom of the stela is a prayer for blessings.

Kemet (Egypt)

Kemet, originally called Chem or Khemet, is the name of the country that we now call Egypt. In spite of scientific evidence and eyewitness accounts of Africans' presence in Kemet thousands of years ago, many people still do not realize that Kemet is in Africa. Many people also don't realize that the founders of Kemet were Black people and that they were the original inhabitants of Africa. Egypt is the name given to Kemet by the Greeks after they conquered the nation. The word Kemet means, "land of the blacks". Some people called it "country of the blacks". **Kemite** (Black) or **Kemtwu** (more than one Black person) is how the people who were born or who lived in Kemet referred to themselves. See the illustrations on the following pages.

Amenhotep III (Known as Amenhotep the Magnificent)
Pharaoh of the 18th Dynasty

Drawing from 18th Dynasty Tomb depicting Black African women

Kemet was one of the world's earliest civilizations that consisted of a way of life centered around culturally diverse people. At the dawn of Kemet's recorded history, there were really two nations called Kemet under the control of separate leaders: Lower Kemet (Egypt) and Upper Kemet (Egypt). These two areas were united around 3,150 B.C. for the first time by a leader named Menes (also referred to as Narma). For the next 3,000 years after Upper Kemet and Lower Kemet became one nation, Narmer continued to practice many of the traditions that were established in Nubia. Also, after he united Upper and Lower Kemet, the Kemetic Kings were depicted in their paintings wearing the "double crown" of Upper and Lower Kemet which represented their union. (See the illustrations on the following page.) The other symbols of Kemetic unity included the papyrus plant of Lower Kemet, the lotus plant of Upper Kemet, the cobra of Lower Kemet and the vulture of Upper Kemet.

Some of Kemet's national symbols are connected to Washington, DC, in Meridian Hill Park which is located on 16th Street, Northwest. For example, the reflection pool that can be found in Meridian Park is adorned with lotus and papyrus plants similar to Kemet's reflection pools and Nile River during ancient times. These plants grew naturally along the Nile River and were used for many practical purposes in Kemetian culture. The United States Park Service maintains and re-plants lotus and papyrus plants every year. (Illustrations of Kemet's national symbols may be seen on the following pages.)

Illustration of individual crowns of Lower Kemet and Upper Kemet and the crown as it appeared when Lower and Upper Kemet united (Double Crown)

Photo by Sya – JNK, CC 2016, British Museum

Amenhotep I wearing the double crown of Upper and Lower Kemet

National symbols of Kemet

Lotus plant of Upper Kemet

Papyrus plant of Lower Kemet

Photo by Erik Hooymans

The Mask of Tutankhamun

The photo above shows the Mask of Tutankhamun's mummy featuring a uraeus from the 18th dynasty. The images of the cobra of Lower Kemet and the vulture of Upper Kemet represent the unification of Lower and Upper Kemet.

Before there were countries, such as Rome, Greece or America, Kemet had already produced tools, literature, mathematics, sciences, musical instruments, and philosophy which are all used today throughout the world. As we journey through this ancient African civilization you bear witness to a documented history of creativity and innovation that spearheaded the production of some of Africa's and the world's greatest treasures. For example, the people of Kemet built **Ipet Isut, one of the world's first centers of education**. Ipet-Isut meant "the holiest of places." It was both a center for religion and education. It housed a brilliant faculty of priest and professors. It has been estimated that at one time there were more than 8,000 students at all grade levels studying at Ipet-Isut University. As with every Kemetian temple or institution of higher learning, Ipet-Isut was staffed with qualified faculty and housed a comprehensive library. The faculty was called "Hersetha" or "Teachers of Mysteries". They were divided into the following departments: Mystery Teachers of 1) astronomy and astrology; 2) geography; 3) geology; 4) philosophy and theology; and, 5) law and communication.

The Kemetian people established the writing system, known as Medu Netcher (hieroglyphics), which was used for thousands of years until it was banned by Emperor Justinian in 550 B.C. Medu Netcher became a lost or forgotten language as a result of this ban but not before they created thousands of books. In addition to their literary contributions, they also created the first documented calendar based on their studies of the constellations and understanding of astronomy. These are just a few of the contributions **Kemtwu** made to Africa and the world from its early origins.

Chapter 2: Agricultural Systems in Kemet

Agriculture is the way people farm land so they can grow crops and breed and **domesticate** animals to provide food, medicine, plants and fiber to sustain and improve life. People in Kemet grew crops, such as barley, wheat, beans and flax, along with fruits and vegetables to eat. During the months from July to September, there were heavy rainfalls. Massive amounts of water flowed into the rivers and rushed downstream into the Nile River and eventually into Kemet's lowlands. This area became known as the **flood plains.** The Kemetians (Ancient Egyptians) used the rich soil from the overflow of the Nile River to **cultivate** the land to grow plants for food and medicine and to sustain animals. But they also used many of the crops they grew in other ways. For example, Egyptian **papyrus**, a plant which is native to Africa, grew along the edges of the Nile River. Kemetians used papyrus to create writing paper, build boats and rafts, create sandals, baskets, mattresses and even produce paper mats to sleep on. It was papyrus that they used to leave us clues about their values, life, education, religious beliefs and family history on what we now refer to as papyrus scrolls.

Both Kushites and Kemetians developed and used agricultural tools. They created these tools to aid them with sowing and growing crops. For example, they used hoes, flails and a manual ploughing system which helped them to prepare the soil during the sowing season. (See an illustration of farmers using manual farming tools on the following page.)

Farmers seeding and using hoes from a scene in the tomb of Nakht near Waset (c.1400 BC)-Francois Guenet

When farmers completed their harvest season, they worked on other projects during the remainder of the year, such as digging canals and assisting in the construction of buildings and monuments.

Photo by Sya -JNK 2016, CC, British Museum

Model of men pounding harvested grains while women baked.

Illustration of Nile River Valley as it appears today.

Gold mines were plentiful in Southern Kemet and Kush and they were a great source of wealth. Both the agricultural system and gold mines allowed leaders of Kemet and Kush to trade goods with other countries which increased their economy. At the same time, gold mines made them a target because it was one of the reasons why some countries constantly tried to invade Kemet. Even today, Africa is considered a high priority for developing strategic partnerships for trade with other nations.

Chapter 3: Kemet's Government

What would a city, state or country look like if there were no one or group of individuals leading it? How would people make decisions about what is best for its citizens? Who would make sure that people were safe and laws were enforced or that buildings and highways were constructed for people to travel and communities established for people to live? How would it organize to educate its citizens and create a **workforce**?

Every civilized nation has people who govern and lead its citizens and Kemet was no different. Leaders are called by different names in different countries. In the United States of America, the person who leads the country is called a president. In England, leaders are called kings and queens. In most history books, leaders of Kemet were referred to as kings, queens and pharaohs. But ancient Kemetians did not use those names to describe themselves or the positions of their leaders. Those names were given to them later by Greek and Roman people who re-named Ancient Kemetians (Egyptians), their artifacts and history. Kemetians called their leaders **Nsw (En-su)**[king] and **Nswt (En-sut)** [queen or empress]. From this point on, I will use the original names created by the people of Kemet.

The Nsw and Nswt made important decisions for their nations. They decided where it was best to dig **irrigation** canals that would result in the best production to feed people. They decided where to erect buildings and monuments and which nations were best for trading goods. They developed statutes that guided the spirituality, or religious beliefs, of citizens. They created libraries that housed books for educating their citizens. These books were later taken and included in the new Library of Alexandria after the Greeks conquered Ancient Egypt (Kemet). It was southern Black African leaders who founded Kemet and ruled it during its golden ages. It was during this time that they experienced significant growth in wealth and power fueled by their own innovation and at times, military force, which allowed them to build their kingdom. Out of thirty ruling dynasties or kingdoms, it was during the first seven dynasties that most of the pyramids were constructed. It was during the 18th dynasty that most of the magnificent temples and tombs were built. It was during the 25th dynasty and after foreign invasions that ancient ways were restored. These were all Black African dynasties.

> **Many of the pioneering structures of Kemet have been buried, moved to other countries, left in ruins weathered from time or defaced by tomb robbers.**

The structures of Kemet represent a time in ancient history that has been forgotten or was never known to many people even though the Kemetian's reign of 30 dynasties lasted approximately 6,000 years. Usually, one family would rule the country for many years.

The diagram on the following page was created by Dr. Asa Hilliard to show how Kemet evolved from its beginning after Lower and Upper Kemet were united by Narmer. Dr. Hilliard was an educational psychologist, professor at San Francisco State and Georgia State Universities, author and historian. He was superintendent of schools in Monrovia, Liberia, founding member of the Association for the Study of Classical African Civilizations, consultant to the Peace Corps and expert witness on test validity and bias.

Kemetic Chronology: A Summary (Dr. Asa Hilliard, III)

KEMETIC CHRONOLOGY
ASA G. HILLIARD, III 1988

3000 BCE	Dynasty 1 — 3100	
	Dynasties 3-6 — 1st Golden Age (Old K.) 2665 - 2160, Pyramid Age	505 YEARS
	1st Intermediate Period (Internal Disorder)	120 YEARS
2000 BCE	**Dynasties 11-12** — 2nd Golden Age (Mid K.) 2040 - 1784, Literary Age	256 YEARS
	2nd Intermediate Period (Hyksos Invasion 1750-1552)	230 YEARS
	Dynasties 18-19 — 3rd Golden Age (New K.) 1554 - 1190, Temple & Imperial Age	364 YEARS
1000 BCE	3rd Intermediate Period	430 YEARS
	Dynasty 25 — 4th Golden Age (Late K.) 760 - 657, Revival Age	103 YEARS
0	Persian Invasion 525 - 405 and 434 - 332 BCE	
	Greek Invasion 332 - 30 BCE	
	Roman Invasion 30 BCE - 395 ACE	
	Arab Invasion 648 ACE	

Although some people were in noble positions, not everyone was born into a family destined to become the next Nsw or Nswt. People in the country had different roles and different jobs just as we do in modern society. Many Kemetians were highly skilled and worked in a variety of trades and professions in addition to those who held noble positions. They were craftsmen, designers, architects, ironmakers, engineers, artists, farmers, philosophers, stonemasons, merchants and civil servants. Together, they built cities, educated their people, and **erected** great monuments, pyramids and statues in honor of their Nsw and Nswt. Some refer to this time as having the first "middle-class" society.

Illustration of artists and other craftsmen.

FUN FACT: Africans were the first brick and stone masons on Earth. One of the buildings they created (The Great Pyramid) was the tallest building in the world for more than 4,000 years.

Review Questions

Read the directions and answer each question below.

1. Explain one of the reasons we know that Kush existed before Kemet.

2. Name three disciplines that Kemtwu developed and studied.

3. Explain how the Nile Valley helped Kemetians with trading and farming.

4. Where does the White Nile and the Blue Nile Rivers meet?

5. How long is the Nile Valley and Nile River?

6. What temple does the Washington Monument resemble? What is the original name given to structures like the Washington Monument by the Kemetian people who created them?

7. What names did Kemetians use to identify their leaders?

8. Dr. John Henry Clarke said the name that people call themselves must provide them with an understanding of their history by connecting them to 5 things. What are those 5 things?

Part Two
Nswt (Queens) of Nile Valley Civilization

Nefertari – Louvre Museum

Chapter 4: Kushite Kingdoms

You will discover:

1. The names of and the relationship between the Kushite Kingdoms
2. How African women became Kendake warriors
3. Nswts of Kemet and Nubia and their roles during the Nile Valley civilization period

Important words to know:

Kendake	Candace	Kemetologist	Kushite Kingdoms
mural	Ethiopia	archaeologist	Diplomat
Kush	Nubia	peace treaty	family tree
mummified	Meroë	obelisk	matriarchal
armana letter	co-regent		

Cities of Antiquity

The Kingdom of **Kush (Nubia)** was located south of Ancient Kemet (Egypt). Most of its cities bordered the Nile River. The Kingdom of Kush actually began at Kerma. Some of the first Queens of the Nile Valley can be traced to **Meroë (Me-ro-wa)**. Meroë, which became the capital of Kush by 500BC, was an ancient city on the east bank of the Nile. It was originally called *Saba*, named after the country's original founder. The city was renamed by Cambyses, a Persian king, to give honor to his sister whose name was Meroë. Meroë had more than two hundred Nubian pyramids and is famous for its more pointed pyramids which served as burial chambers for its queens and kings. These structures once stood tall as a testament to the Kushites' mastery of architecture; but, today many are damaged.

Kush was a wealthy empire due to resources such as gold and iron which they used to trade. They were pioneers in creating iron for warfare, such as iron blades and spears, which enabled them to maintain a strong military to defend their kingdom and its lucrative resources. The strategic foresight of creating such weapons to stand apart from other kingdoms and nations during that time that did not possess the skill and resources to create this type of weaponry would prove valuable to the Kushites in their defense of the Kingdom of Kush against the Roman military.

Meroitic pyramids, Wikimedia Commons

Nubian pyramids were built by the rulers of the ancient Kushite kingdoms.

The area of the Nile valley known as Nubia (Kush) which we refer to as Sudan today, was home to three **Kushite kingdoms:** Meroë, Napata and Kerma. In 751 B.C.E., the Kushite King Piankhi overthrew the 24th Dynasty and **united** the entire Nile Valley from the delta to the city of Napata under his rule. Piankhi and his descendants ruled as the Nsw of the 25th dynasty.

At the time of their exploration by archaeologists in the 19th and 20th centuries, some pyramids were found to contain the remains of bows, quivers of arrows, horse harnesses, wooden boxes, furniture, pottery, colored glass, metal vessels, and many other artifacts. Historians believe that these artifacts confirm the extensive trades between Meroë, Kemet (Egypt) and other parts of the world.

Photo by Anthony T. Browder, 2016

Nubian pyramids at Meroë

Photo by Anthony T. Browder, 2016

Nubian pyramids at Meroë

Chapter 5: Kendakes from the Kingdom of Kush (Nubia)

The Four Kendakes

While there are many Kendakes (ken-da-ke) documented in African history, there were some who were most memorable and impressive because of their powerful leadership and contributions in safeguarding the Kingdom of Kush. Many historians and archaeologists have written about these warrior women and documented their historical contributions which were immense in maintaining stability and order in the nation. The Kendakes were known to rule with an Nsw (King) but more often, they ruled independently, or as a stand-alone Nswt (Queen Mother). They developed a fierce reputation for military leadership that eventually caused some potential foreign invaders to yield rather than to battle and risk great loss. There are many images of Kendakes painted on murals or etched in stone showing their bravery in defending their nation as well as documentation in Roman records. In addition to the Roman's recordation, the Kushite people provided a direct account of these historical events written in meroitic script on a stela from the second half of the 1st century during the reign of Kendake Amanirenas. Historians have deciphered the writing system but still find the language difficult to interpret. With time and technology, their work continues to bring greater understanding of this significant time in history.

There were some Kendakes who stood out and are documented in history as the "The Four Kendakes" whom we will discuss more in the following sections. Let's take a look into their origins and learn why they were given this title.

Origins of Kendakes: From Queens to Warriors

African Nswt (Queens) are often depicted as beautiful women adorned in precious stones and jewelry. They ensured that the family line continued and were responsible for the care of the family. They also had other significant roles. Did you know that women led and fought in military warfare in Ancient Kemet (Egypt) and other African countries over 8,000 years ago? The women who assumed this role were called **matriarchal warriors**. A look at history will reveal that they fought admirably although not necessarily by choice but rather out of necessity and obligation to their nation. These female warriors were soon known as "Kendakes" but they were also called Nubian Warriors, Queen Mothers and Queen Regents. They were from the Royal House of Kush (Nubia) and they were known for ruling independent of a King. The rulership was passed from one woman to another; or, from the Queen to her son or daughter.

Much of the information we know about the Kendakes is based on artifacts from their temples and tombs as well as meroitic scripts. Based on those findings, they were thought to be powerful and strategic leaders. One Queen Mother, Kendake Aminatore, was considered to be a powerful leader of her army, an avid builder who commissioned more temples than any other Nubian ruler and the builder of reservoirs to retain water. Archaeologists uncovered many artifacts, including her crown. Her artifacts suggest that she was a large woman like some other Kendakes. This may be observed in a carving on her temple where she towers over a captured invader. Eventually, the Romans changed the name of these women from Kendake, or Kentakes, to **Candace (Can-da-ce)**.

Commons by Istvánka using CommonsHelper., CC BY-SA 3.0

The relief on the right pylon of the Apedemak Temple depicting Queen Amanitore smiting her enemies.

Amanitore at Wad ban Naqa]

Pyramid (Mir) of Amanitore

There were many queen mothers who were considered to be among the kendakes of Meroe. As historians and archaeologists continue their efforts to uncover artifacts about this time period and these great women of history, we may learn even more about their vast contributions. Some of the kendakes who we have located evidence for include the following list of women:

Kendake Ruler	**Rulership Time Period**
Shanakdakhete	[c. 177 BCE - 155 BCE]
Amanirenas	[c. 40 BCE – 10 BCE]
Amanishakheto	[c. 10 BCE – 1 CE]
Amanitore	[c. 1- 20 CE]
Amantitere	[c. 25 – 41 CE]
Amanikhatashan	[c. 62 – 85 CE]
Maleqorobar	[c. 266 – 283 CE]
Lahideamani	[c. 306 – 314 CE]

The Four Kendakes

Now that you know about the origins of the Kendakes, let us look more closely at "The Four Kendakes" who received even greater attention for their leadership and contributions to Nubia. **The four Kendakes were Amanishakheto** (A-mani-shu-ke-to)**, Amanirenas** (A-mani-re-nas)**, Nawidemak** (Na-wi-de-mok) **and Malesgereabar** (Ma-les-ger-a-bar).

Kendake Amanishakheto

Amanishakheto was the daughter of Kendake Amanirenas and the mother of Kendake Amanitore. She is considered to be one of the most prosperous Kendakes based on the success of the country during her reign and the massive amount of riches that were found in her temples. Although historians are still attempting to learn more about her and other Kendakes, when her temple was uncovered there were many artifacts that showed us who she was and how she lead her people. For example, there are artifacts that show her carrying bows and arrows. Some **murals** show Kendake Amanishakheto with prisoners she had captured during military warfare tied up.

Amanishakheto's artifacts were found by an Italian explorer, Giuseppe Ferlini, who went to Nubia (present day Sudan) in search of gold. His team discovered her pyramid and a hidden chamber that was full of artifacts wrapped in linen, including a significant amount of jewelry such as the bracelet shown on the following page. Many of her artifacts are currently located in the Cairo Museum. There is also a portrait of her in the Amun Temple in Kawa.

Photo by Sven-Steffen Arndt - Own work, CC BY-SA 2.0,

Bracelet from the tomb of Kendake Amanishakheto

Kendake Amanirenas

Several Nswt (Queens) have ruled Kush, but many historians agree that one of the greatest is certainly Amanirenas. Ruling for about 30 years, she is best known for leading her forces against the Romans attempted invasions of Egypt. Kendake Amanirenas ruled at a time when Nubia was constantly threatened by the Roman empire. She led armies into battles defeating the Roman armies on at least three separate occasions over a five year period of time. On one such occasion, she prepared a military of 30,000 to wage a war which caused Roman Augustus Caesar to retreat from his plan to attack when he and his men arrived and saw her army. This occurred after the Roman military had defeated territories in

Britain, the middle East and other parts of Africa. Yet, Amanirenas returned to Kush with treasures and some prisoners she acquired resulting from the wars against the Romans. She also returned with a bronze bust of the head of Emperor Augustus Caesar. She placed the bust under her grand temple allowing all who visited the temple to walk over him. After her successes, the Romans continued to pushed back. In 23BC, Amanirenas strategic prowess allowed her to negotiate a peace treaty which was signed in favorable terms for Kush, guaranteeing their freedom and independence for 400 years.

Claud Angus - Black Articultral Art.
Amanirenas

Kendake Nawidemak

There is not much documentation on Nawidemak but we do know that she was a ruling Queen Mother during the 1st Century BC. Her rulership status is based on artifacts found in her chapel, such as a royal coat, sash and tasselcord. Those were associated with male rulers of that period.

These Queen Mothers all demonstrated unique abilities to manage the nation, negotiate trades that increased wealth for the country, commission ongoing building of the cities, monuments and pyramids based on their traditions and lead men in wars to protect their country. There are many images of Kendakes painted on **murals** or etched in stone showing their bravery in defending their nation.

Chapter 6: Queens of Kemet

What would you say if I told you that Kemetian women had the right to vote thousands of years ago? Would you consider the possibility that Kemetian women had what we would consider professional jobs as doctors, judges and roles in government? Evidence documented in history tells us that they did. In fact, women played a critical part of building Kemet in partnership, or in conjunction, with their male counterparts. Some historians suggest that there were women in Kemet who should be considered among the greatest leaders of all the dynasties. It is also fascinating to learn that over thousands of years ago, Kemetian women had the right to own property, to have occupations, and to fight and lead in the military. Women were recognized as a part of the political process, exercising their right to vote. To put this accomplishment into perspective, women did not begin to vote in the United States of America in 1920.

Women participated in society and contributed their knowledge and skills in a variety of occupations. For example, **one of the world's first documented female physicians was Peseshet, who practiced medicine during the 4th dynasty around 2,500B.C.** She was called the Lady Overseer of the Lady Physicians. The tablet on the following page shows some of the instruments Peseshet used in her medical practice.

Tablet showing medical instruments used by Peseshet circa 2500.

Today, if you visit Kemet you will see huge statues and tombs that were built to honor some of Kemet's Nswt. Let's explore the lives of some of these women who stand out based on their exemplary leadership records starting with Nswt Nefertari (Ne-fer-ta-re).

Fun Facts:

Wigs and some hair care accessories are not new. Many Africans wore them thousands of years ago. Below is a picture of some of the wigs (artifacts) found which are now located in museums.

African American woman in Cairo museum observing wigs worn by Ancient Kemetian women.

Photo by Sya – JNK 2016 CC, British Museum

Combs, commonly known as "picks" today were used by Africans in Nubia and Kemet.

Nswt Nefertari

Photo illustration by Maler Grabkammer

Tomb wall depicting Queen Nefertari

Nswt Nefertari is known as the Great Royal Wife of Nsw Ramesses II. Her name means "the most beautiful" or "beautiful companion". Nefertari had many sons and daughters with her husband, Rameses. They were considered to be the royal family. Nefertari served as a diplomat, communicating with leaders and rulers of other nations as an equal. In her honor, Ramesses had a temple constructed called, Abu Simbel. It is located on the west side of the Nile River and includes two temples. One temple has four huge statues of Ramesses. Another temple pays tribute by showing two statues depicting Nefertari at the entrance way in addition to four of Ramesses. These temples and statues were all carved into the mountain. They were not built out of stones like many others. (See illustration on the following page).

There are beautiful paintings that tell us stories about the life and times of Nefertari and Ramesses which reveals some of the things that we could infer were important to them during their reign. It is through this art and custom that historians, archaeologists, and **Kemetologists** were able to learn so much about them. This was how the Kemetians were able to preserve and share their beliefs, customs and culture with us.

Abu Simbel – Two rock temples built by Ramesses II during his reign from 1279 to 1213 BCE

Nswt Hatshepsut

Did you know that almost all Nsw wore a false beard? During that time, a beard was a symbol of power. As such, this was generally reserved for Nsw but one of the Nswt wore a false beard to show that she ruled the country as an equal and was as powerful as any of the Nsw. Nswt Hatshepsut (Hat-shep-sut) was so well-respected among her peers and citizens that she was called and honored as a Pharaoh (King versus Queen). She was also one of the longest ruling females in Ancient Egypt ruling for 20 years during the 15th century B.C.

Illustration of Hapshetsut with false beard.

Hatshepsut was responsible for improving international relationships which allowed her to expand foreign trades. She also created and maintained a strong military, especially the navy. She is known for her work in building and restoring monuments in Kemet and Nubia. Under her leadership, skilled craftsmen repaired buildings and created new ones that were called temples. Hatshepsut built several **tekhenu (obelisks). A tekhen is a tapered four-sided pillar used for measuring shadow length, usually inscribed with Medu Ntr (hieroglyphs) proclaiming the achievements** of a Nsw. The Greeks called them "obelisks" (o-be-lisks). The ancient Kemetian people who built them called them "tekhen" (tek-hen) for a single one, "tekhenw" (tek-he-nw) for two and a "tekhenwy" for 3 or more. Some of the obelisks were more than 100 feet tall. One of the obelisks she had constructed was Zosert-Zosru which means, "holiest of holy places". It is now called "Dier el-Bahari.

Temple of Hatshepsut (Zosert – Zosru *"The Holy of Holies"*)

Photo by Olaf Tausch

Fallen Tekhen (obelisk)

Photos by Sya – JNK, 2016 CC, British Museum

Pink granite tekhen for Nswt Hapshepsut. One side describes her as "beloved of Horus" but names were destroyed allegedly to erase her from history.

FUN FACT:

Kemetians (Egyptians) wore purple on special occasions because they considered it to be a sacred color. People who were considered royalty and hose who were a part of the priesthood only wore purple during these special occasions.

Nswt Tiye

Photo by Einsamer Schütze - Own work, CC BY-SA 3.0

Nswt (Queen) Tiye, Ägyptisches Museum (Egyptian Museum), Berlin

Nswt Tiye, who was originally from Nubia, ruled Kemet alongside her husband, Amenhotep III, during the 18th dynasty. Remember, **a dynasty is a period of time that a family ruled, or lead, the country**.

Photo by Rama - Own work, CC BY-SA 2.0 fr

Nswt (Queen) Tiye

Tiye changed the way that women were treated in Kemet. She was admired for her beauty, intelligence, independent style for fashion and her ability to lead Kemet as a coregent with her husband. She also ruled independently when the time came for her to do so. He made her his **coregent** (equal partner) which allowed her to attend to matters of the country along with him as an equal. Amenhotep III publicly displayed his love and affection for Tiye during a time when it was not the tradition. He disregarded the tradition of having the wife placed beside the knee of the husband on honorary structures and instead he built statues of him and his queen of equal height sitting next to each other. As a result of this, Tiye became involved with **international relations** (building good relationships with leaders of other countries) and was highly respected for her knowledge and advice in areas of foreign relations.

After her son, Amenhotep IV, became Nsw upon the death of his father, he spent a great deal of his time focused on his religious interests. Kemet's military status began to decline. Because Tiye had been coregent with her husband, she recognized the decline and began to act as Secretary of State. Kings of other nations recognized and respected Tiye's intelligence and political knowledge. They came to her and requested political and military protection. One of Tiye's most well-known accomplishments was the Amarna Letters. They were discovered in 1887.

> **Amarna Letters are clay tablets used for writing and communications between foreign kings and the Egyptian pharaohs.**

Photo by Sya - JNK, 2016 CC, British Museum

Armana Letters on clay tablets.

The photo above captures three letters which were taken from a palace archive at el-Amarn from Tushratta, Nsw (king) of Mitanni. The letters were written to Nsw Amenhotep III and Nswt Tiye to document trading of gold and other gifts.

Amenhotep III

Nswt Tiye's husband, Amenhotep III

FUN FACT:

Nswt Tiye's Dynasty included well-known leaders who contributed greatly to the progression of Kemet. See her **family tree** below.

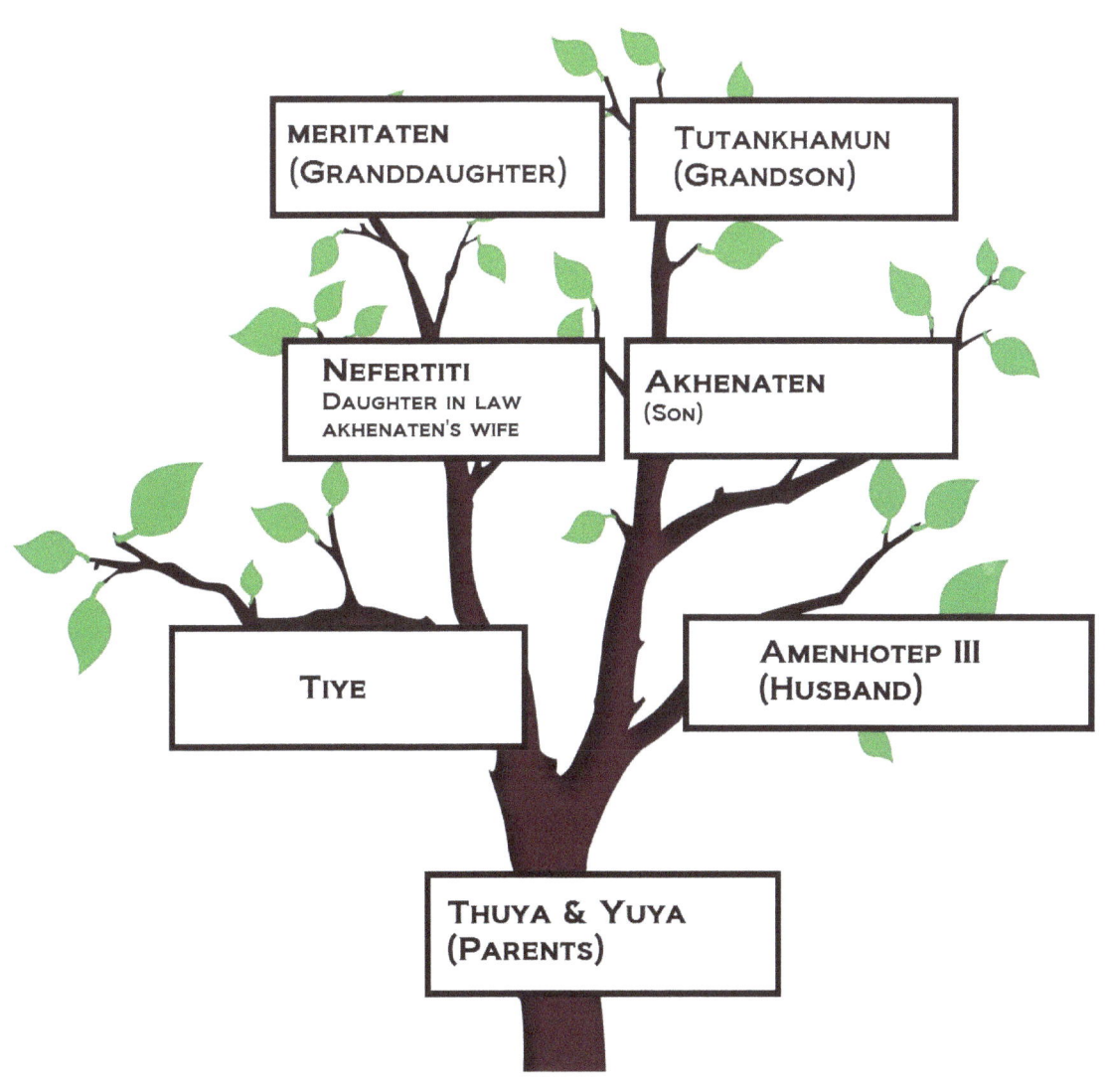

Photo credit: mathstat.slu.edu

This picture depicts Princess Meritaten standing behind her parents, Akhenaten and Nefertiti. Meritaten was actually the oldest of three children. In the photo above, her younger sisters, Meketaten and Ankhesenpaaten, follows behind her.

ca. 1390-1352 B.C.E. Wood, gold leaf, 10 1/4 x 1 7/8 x 5 1/2 in. (26 x 4.8 x 14 cm)
Brooklyn Museum, Charles Edwin Wilbour Fund, 54.187. Creative Commons-BY (Photo: Brooklyn Museum, 54.187_front_PS2.jpg)

Standing Statuette of Lady Tuty, 18th Dynasty

FUN FACT:

Certain elements—such as the big gilded earrings and the faint traces of gilded sandals—associate her with the extraordinary wealth of Amenhotep's time. The cone on her head represents a type of perfumed ointment worn by the wealthy at banquets and other opulent occasions. The cone gradually melted, releasing its fragrance over the hair and clothes.

Review Questions

1. Name at least 3 facts about Meroë.
2. Explain why Africa had matriarchal warriors and explain their role. How does it compare to women's roles in the military today?
3. The Greeks changed the Kendakes' name. What was the new name?
4. Name 1 Nswt of Kemet, list 3-5 facts about her and explain why you selected to report on her.
5. Who was the first documented female physician?

Research Activity

Using the internet and other resources, find out more information about one of the Nswt listed below. List 3 facts that you think are important for people to know and explain why.

1. **Princess Meritaten (Merit-aten)** (18th Dynasty)
2. **Nswt Hetepheres I** (4th Dynasty)
3. **Nswt Candace** (Empress of Ethiopia)

Part Three

Some Kings of Nile Valley Civilization:

Nubia and Kemet

Photo by Anthony Browder, 2016

Chapter 7: Pharaohs of High Culture

You will discover:

1. Information about Nsw and their role in Kemet
2. The Nsw who was responsible for the construction of Abu Simbel and the world's oldest pyramid (**mir** - original name for pyramid).
3. The Table of Abydos and its importance to Kemetcian culture

Important words to know:

mummy	Table of Abydos	diplomacy
quarried	Temple of Karnak	mir
mastabas	Great Pyramid	invade
skyscraper	Renovate	reign

Nsw (Kings and Pharaohs) played significant roles in the creation and developments throughout Ancient Egypt and, subsequently, the world. They constructed cities, established laws and systems and led trading and mining expeditions that laid the groundwork for the civilization. They led their people and country by making sure that they had a strong military to fight foreigners who tried to **invade** Kemet. They built the **Great Pyramid** at Giza Plateau, the **Luxor Temple** and Her-em-akhet. They demonstrated their knowledge of the high sciences in the structures which they had erected throughout Kemet. For example, it is fascinating that Her-em-akhet (The Great Sphinx) was carved from one single rock. The monument, with the head of a human and the body of a lion, is 240 feet long and 66 feet high. The Great Pyramid was so large that it has been said to have used enough stones to build 33 Empire State buildings.

> **The Great Pyramid is the last of the Seven Wonders of the World still standing today.**

African Nsw also introduced agriculture, showed **diplomacy** and increased economic levels within their countries by trading goods with other nations. They recognized that they needed to create and maintain good relationships with other countries. This skill aided them in increasing wealth for Kemet. They studied and showed a great respect for the Earth and other planets. They followed the laws and rules of nature to determine their values and establish their way of life. Kemetian leaders believed in using signs from the Earth and Universe to live in harmony with nature.

Narmer

Nsw Horus Narmer-Menes was the Nsw (King) of the first dynasty of Kemet. He was responsible for uniting lower and upper Kemet into one country. During the early dynastic period, countries had capitals of states just as we do today. After Narmer brought Lower Kemet and Upper Kemet together he declared Memphis as the capital of Kemet. Memphis was to Kemet what Washington, DC is to the United States of America – the central location for the administration of government. For Kemet, it was also the core to religious, or spiritual training and the foundation for every aspect of Kemetic life.

FUN FACT:

The King of Kemet lived in a painted brick palace which was constructed within a "White Wall". Since it was a white house built within white walls, the Kemetic people referred to it as the "Double White House". As you know, the USA President's home is also referred to as "The White House."

Taharqa

Nsw Taharqa (Tir-ha-kah) was the last Kushite (Nubian) ruler of Kemet. He is also the only Nsw whose name is mentioned in the Bible as King Tirhakah of Ethiopia (Pharaoh of the 25th dynasty). Taharqa spent a considerable amount of his time with his army fighting the Assyrians before finally establishing peace. Once he was able to keep the Assyrians away, he used that time to re-energize and **renovate** the country. Taharqa's craftsmen restored many of the temples and pyramids that were damaged. He restored the temple Amon-Ra at Jebel Barkal. He also built the oldest and largest pyramid that was ever erected in Napata or the surrounding areas.

Source: Unknown

Djoser

Nsw Djoser ruled during the 3rd dynasty. **His statue is the oldest known life-sized statue that archaeologists have found to date**. One of his most well-known accomplishments was the monument that Imhotep, his engineer and chief priest, designed –the step pyramid. Its design was new and consisted of building **mastabas/steps** on top of one another. A step pyramid is an architectural structure that uses flat platforms, or steps, receding from the ground up to achieve a completed shape similar to a geometric pyramid. It is the world's first **skyscraper.**

Photo By Jon Bodsworth

Limestone statue of Djoser (Egyptian Museum in Cairo)

Ramesses II

Nsw Ramesses II ruled Kemet during the 19th Dynasty for more than 60 years after starting his reign during his teen years. He is known as "Ramesses the Great" for many reasons. Ramesses' father was Nsw Seti I. Upon Seti's death, Rameses assumed the throne as the 3rd Nsw of the 19th Dynasty of Kemet. Ramesses built many well-known structures, including the Ramesseum. Some of his other structures were in observance of his family and those he completed in honor of his father, such as the Great Hypostyle Hall at Karnak.

By the time Ramesses completed his **reign**, he had built more than any other leader throughout Kemet and Nubia. This may be one of the reasons he is considered one of the most widely known "pharaohs" of Ancient Egypt (Kemet).

Photo by Sya – JNK, CC 2016 British Museum

Pharaoh Ramesses II

Photo by Than217 at English Wikipedia

The Nefertari Temple at Abu Simbel commemorates Ramesses II and his Queen wife, Nefertari. It also commemorates his victory during the Battle of Kadesh.

Nsw Seti Meryenptah I, 19th Dynasty

By Messuy at French Wikipedia -Photo by Messuy, CC BY-SA 3.0

Image of Seti I from Temple of Abydos constructed 1300BC

Nsw Seti (Se-ti) was a ruler during the 19th Dynasty. He was also the father of Ramesses the Great. Seti I ruled Ancient Egypt from 1290 B.C. to 1279 B.C.

Pharaoh Seti was known for his contributions in the architecture of Kemet. He was responsible for building the **Great Temple of Abydos (A-by-dos) in 1300 B.C**. Although he did not complete the temple, his son, Ramesses the Great, did finish the temple in his honor.

Photo by Roland Unger, CC BY-SA 3.0

Great Temple of Abydos

Abydos is one of the oldest cities in Ancient Egypt. Its construction began during the reign of Nswt Seti I around 1318-1304 BC and it was finished during the reign of his son, Ramses II (1304-1237 BC)

Seti also created the **Table of Abydos.** The Table of Abydos is important because it is a list that contains the names of 76 pharaohs who ruled during the seventh and eighth ancient dynastic periods. After it was discovered it became known as **'the King's List"**.

Photos by Sya – JNK, CC 2016 British Museum

Detailed view of the Table of Abydos (King's List) which contains the names of 76 kings and pharaohs from the ancient dynastic period.

Seti died in 1279 B.C. When they discovered his tomb, there were many works of art on the walls of the tomb. Tombs from that period were often damaged or destroyed by robbers but his was not. It is located in the Valley of the Kings/Valley of the Queens. His **mummy** is presently in the Egyptian Museum of Cairo.

Tuthmosis IV

Nsw Tuthmosis IV (Tuth-mo-sis) ruled Egypt between 1419 B.C. and 1386 B.C. His father was Amenhotep II, another great King of Kemet. Tuthmosis built a giant obelisk that was originally **quarried** at Aswan under Tuthmosis III, his grandfather. **Quarried means to dig into the ground for rocks.** Tuthmosis's tekhen was the tallest obelisk that we know about. It was 105 feet tall. It stands at the **Temple of Karnak**. He also restored, or repaired, the **Sphinx at Giza Plateau.**

Photo by Iry-Hor - Own work, CC BY-SA 3.0
Musee du Louvre in Paris

Thutmose IV

Sarcophagus of King Tutankhamun

Illustration of "King Tut" (Curt Cunningham)

FUN FACT:

Known throughout history as "King Tut", he became King as a young boy after the death of his father, Pharaoh Akhenaten. As a result of artifacts discovered in his tomb, historians were able to capture a view of family life among nobles. More recently, scientists have performed tests using DNA technology to learn more about him.

Source: http://africanknowledge.weebly.com/the-egyptians.html

King Tutankhamun known as "King Tut"

There were many other Nsw (kings/ pharaohs) who ruled Kemet and Kush. I shared some of them with you. You can learn more about some others using the list below:

1. Amenhotep II
2. Ahmose
3. Khafra
4. Menkare
5. **Unas**
6. **Shabaka**
7. **Kashta**

Photo by Sya – JNK, CC 2016, British Museum

Statue of Amenhotep with Medu Netcher that contains a prayer for his continued existence in the hereafter. This statue was placed in the temple of Osiris which was located in Abydos.

Review Questions

Read the directions and answer the questions below.

1. Why was the Table of Abydos so important? What name was later given to this artifact?
2. What structure is considered to be the world's first skyscraper?
3. Fill in the blanks:

   _____ united Upper and Lower Kemet. He was considered to be the Nsw (King) of the ___ Dynasty.
4. Research three of the kings listed on page 87 and find out the following information:

   a. When did they begin and end their reign?

   b. Describe one significant contribution they made during their reign.

5. What was the role of Nsw (kings/pharaohs)? How does it compare to the role of the US President or other leaders in modern society?
6. What is the King's List and who is credited with creating it? What kind of information can we learn from the King's List?

Part Four
Imhotep

Photo Credit: wikipedia commons. (n.d.). Imhotep louvre. Retrieved from https://commons.wikimedia.org/wiki/File:Imhotep-Louvre.jpg

Chapter 8: The World's First Multi-Genius

You will discover:

1. Why Imhotep was considered the world's first multi-genius, father of medicine and father of architecture
2. Some of the arts and sciences that Imhotep mastered
3. How the Hippocratic Oath got its name

Important words to know

vizier	scribe	Hippocratic Oath	astronomer
astrologer	silt	antiseptic	sage
deity	philosopher	equator	Edwin Smith Papyrus

Designer of the Step Pyramid

> **Imhotep is known as the world's first multi-genius.**

Imhotep is the earliest known engineer, philosopher, physician, architect, scribe and astronomer. Many people also refer to him as the world's first multi-genius! His name means "He who comes in peace". Imhotep was also a priest, **sage** poet, astrologer, **vizier** and chief minister to Nsw Djoser who reigned from 2630 to 2611 BC as the second Nsw of Kemet's third dynasty.

Designer of Step Pyramid Complex

Imhotep was the world's first named architect. He was commissioned to build the world's first documented stone structure. Imhotep's pyramid, known as the Step Pyramid, is located at the Grand Lodge of Djoser in Sakkara near the present day city of Cairo. At 197 feet tall, it was the largest building in the world for thousands of years. The pyramids that were built before Imhotep's were built using two other methods known in Sudan. One method used mudbricks and the second method was called silt pyramids.

Photo by Charlesjsharp - Own work, from Sharp Photography, sharpphotography, CC BY-SA 3.0

Saqqara pyramid of Djoser in Egypt

Photo credit: Anthropology.msu.edu

Step Pyramid Complex (Saqqara)

Father of Medicine

Imhotep was recognized as the **father of medicine.** Many men learned about this art of healing from Imhotep. He found cures to diseases, vaccinations and **antiseptics** that could clean wounds and prevent infections. He also performed advanced surgeries. Approximately 2200 years later, Hippocrates, Europe's first physician, wrote what has become known as the **Hippocratic Oath**. In this oath, he referenced Imhotep whom the Greeks re-named "Asclepius". That oath is still used today when physicians complete training and swear to use good practice and judgment with patients. It is called the Hippocratic Oath in honor of Hippocrates. In his own words documented in the Hippocratic Oath, he wrote that he had a god named Asclepius, the Greek name for the God (deity) Imhotep. Imhotep died more than 2,500 years before Hippocrates was born. However, because Hippocrates was Europe's first physician and the Hippocratic Oath is used in the medical profession today, most people believe that Hippocrates is the Father of Medicine and the first physician. Imhotep is named as being the author of the **Edwin Smith Papyrus** (named after the person who bought it around 1862) which is the earliest creditable book on medicine that is based on science. This scroll described 48 cases of injuries, such as wounds, fractures and even tumors.

<u>Hippocratic Oath</u>: I swear by Apollo, the physician, and Asclepius and Health and All Heal and all the gods and goddess that, according to my ability and judgment, I will keep this oath and stipulation
.

Photo by Sya – JNK,CC 2016

Caduceus – Symbol used to represent the medical field in the USA

Review Questions

Read the directions and answer the questions below.

1. List 3 titles assigned to Imhotep. Explain why you believe he earned each title.

2. Discuss the Hippocratic Oath. Who wrote it? Why was Imhotep mentioned and by what name was he called when it was written? How is the Hippocratic Oath used today?

Activity: Using the internet, search "Hippocratic Oath" and read it in its entirety.

3. Name and describe the three methods architects used to build pyramids.

Part Five: Architectural Masterpieces of Kemet

Aerial view of Giza pyramid complex   Photo by Robster1983 at English Wikipedia

Photo by Sya – JNK, CC 2016

The London Needle is in Westminster, London near the Golden Jubilee Bridges. It was originally erected in Ancient Egypt by Nsw Thutmose III.

Chapter 9: Magnificent Structures Built in Nubia and Kemet

You will discover:

1. Some of the largest and oldest architectural structures in the world
2. How Kemetian people used the solar system and physics to build temples
3. How modern researchers are discovering new artifacts from Ancient Kemet

Important words to know:

excavation	Restoration
Pyramid of Khafre	Pyramid of Menkure
Pyramid of Khufu	Equator
Great Step Pyramid of Djoser	

Pyramids, Tekhen (Obelisks) and Temples

One might wonder where the Kemetic people got their vision and skills for architecture. They continue to be at the forefront of having developed some of the most astounding structures in the world. Many of the teknwu, pyramids and temples conceived and erected have been duplicated in many other countries. Teknwu originally found in Ancient Kemet can easily be connected to structures erected thousands of years later, such as Rome, Istanbul, Paris, London, New York, Berlin and Vatican City in addition to the monument located in Washington, DC. History shows that there were well over 1,200 tekhenwy erected in Kemet during its ancient period but there are only approximately 12 that stands in Egypt now. The construction of some temples and pyramids in Kemet were more complex. Even today, archaeologists and Egyptologists still have questions about how they built some of them and are still undergoing research to advance their knowledge in this area. Many of the pyramids built by Kemetian people still exist today but others were either intentionally damaged or naturally damaged by time and nature through the years.

The Great Pyramid is composed of approximately two and one half million stones which weigh an average of two and one-half tons each. Its base covers an area of 13.11 square acres or seven city blocks. There are more stones in the Great Pyramid than all the cathedrals, churches and chapels built in England since the time of Christ. It equals the height of a 45 story building and has enough stones to build 33 Empire State buildings. It is so large that if all of the stones were cut into one foot blocks and laid from beginning to end, they would stretch two-thirds of the distance around the Earth at the **equator**. This pyramid was built by skilled masons, not slaves as some may mistakenly believe. The way pyramids and temples were built shows us how much Kemetians knew about the universe. For example, Ramesses II built Abu Simbel to honor himself and his wife, Nefertari. Every year on October 22 and February 22, the sun shines through the front entrances and lands on the face of the statues in the back of the temple. The Kemetians understood the solar system and physics to build the temple and place the statues in order for this to occur at a specific place, height and time of day. Similarly, it was Benjamin Banneker, one of the first African American scientists in the USA, who used astronomy and geometry to research information about the rising and setting of the sun, moon and planets. Using his research, he predicted the eclipse of the sun and this data was later used by Andrew Ellicott and Pierre L'Enfant in the design of Washington, DC and many of its temples and buildings on 16th Street.

Temples on 16th Street, NW, Washington, DC known as "church row".

The three largest pyramids are the **Pyramid of Khafre**, the **Pyramid of Menkure** and the **Great Pyramid of Khufu**. Kemetians built pyramids to house the tomb of their Nsw when they were elevated to the position. They invested a great amount of time to make sure that scribes, artists and other skilled craftsmen documented the walls of the pyramid and that the tomb included items that were important to the Nsw.

Photo by MusikAnimal - Own work, CC BY-SA 3.0,

Pyramid of Khafre

CC BY SA 2.5

Pyramid of Menkare

Photo by Nina - Own work, CC BY 2.5

Pyramid of Khufu

As mentioned earlier, Imhotep built the **Step Pyramid of Djoser**. But, Kemetians also built many other pyramids as a way to honor their ancestors. They used it to tell their stories – who they were and how they lived -with beautiful artwork on the tombs that were placed beneath some pyramids. It is through this art and other artifacts they left behind that we continue to learn so much about them and the connection to Africans throughout the world. Some of the pyramids are still there while others have been damaged or destroyed.

Excavating Kemet's Structures in Modern Times

One person who has devoted his professional career to uncovering artifacts and the true history of people of African ancestry is Anthony T. Browder. Browder is an author, publisher, cultural historian, artist, and an educational consultant. He is the founder and director of **IKG Cultural Resources** and has devoted 30 years researching ancient Egyptian history, science, philosophy and culture.

Browder is currently the director of the **ASA Restoration Project**, which is funding the **excavation** and **restoration** of the 25th dynasty tomb of Karakhamen in Luxor, Egypt along with Dr. Elena Pischikova. Can you imagine participating in this type of archaeological project today? What types of artifacts do you think might be uncovered during the excavation?

Browder is the first African American to coordinate an archaeological dig in Egypt. He has lead five archaeological missions to Egypt since 2009. After three decades of study in Egypt, West Africa, South Africa and Mexico, he concluded that ancient Africans were the architects of civilization and that they developed the rudiments of what has become the scientific, religious, and philosophical backbone of mankind.

Photo by Anthony T. Browder, July 2016

Browder during one of his excavation trips to Egypt standing in front of a pyramid

Fun Fact:

Two lion heads are often built on each side of a temple in many countries today. This was an ancient Kemetic practice. The lion on the left symbolized yesterday; the lion on the right symbolized tomorrow. Together, they represented the keepers of yesterday, today and tomorrow.

Browder and his daughter, Atlantis, approximately forty feet below ground under the painted ceiling of Karakhamun's burial chamber.

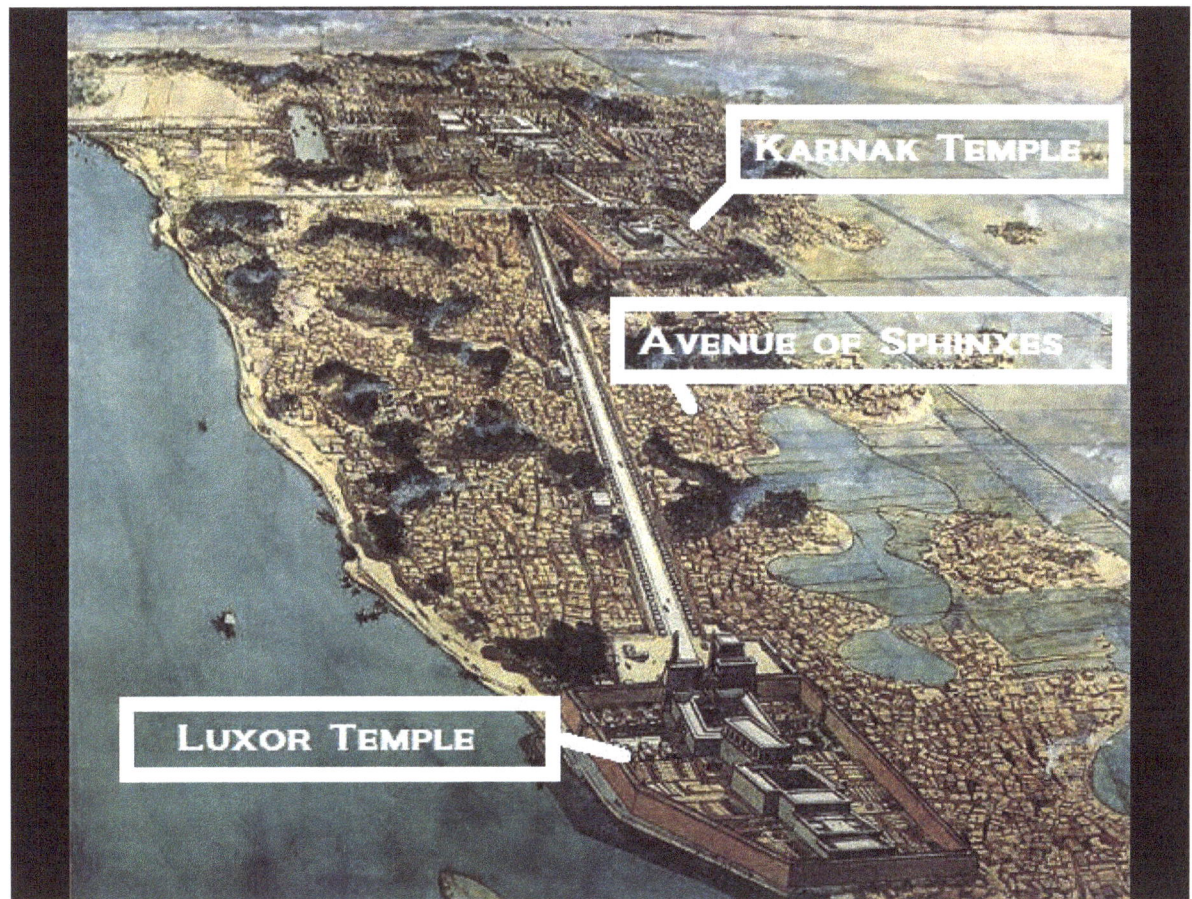

An illustration of Karnak and Luxor Temples on the East Bank of the Nile River

Fun Fact:

The Great Pyramid of Khufu was the tallest structure in the world for 4,250 years until the Washington Monument was built in the USA in 1884 and surpassed it. The Washington Monument is 555 feet tall.

Review Questions

Read the directions and answer each question below.

1. Fill in the circle for the true statement:

- ○ All of the pyramids and teknwu built in Kemet are still standing today because they were well-preserved.

- ○ The Great Pyramid consists of about 2-1/2 million stones.

- ○ The biggest pyramids are the Pyramid of Khafre, Pyramid of Menkare and the Great Pyramid of Khufu.

2. Explain why many historians believe that Abu Simbel which Ramesses II built to honor his wife, Nefertari, is unique.

3. List 3 facts about Anthony Browder. Discuss why his work is valuable today.

4. There are three tekhenwy that were removed from Ancient Egypt in addition to the London Needle on page 96. Using the internet, find out where the other two were taken. **TIP:** Cleopatra's Needle

Part Six

Kemet's Educational System

Chapter 10: Educating a Nation of People in Ancient Times

You will discover:

1. How children were taught during early Nile Valley civilization
2. How Mdr Ntw was developed as the first written language
3. Why and how Ancient Kemetians sought MA'AT

Important words to know:

colonization	mason	Virtue
fossil	cultural unity	social responsibility
apprenticeship	harmonious	Initiates
contradiction	character	moral compass

Origins of Kemet's Educational Systems

As Anthony T. Browder reminds us in his book, *Egypt on the Potomac*, "the word **mason** is derived from the Latin words *mass* and *son*. It literally means "Child of Light," and expresses the desire to pursue "light", a metaphor for the sun that symbolizes knowledge. The term "Child of light" was first used to identify students who had completed 42 years of study in the temples of Kemet." People in Kemet actually did study for a total of 42 years. Can you imagine taking 42 years to complete your education?

Today, when students complete their education, we call them high school or college graduates. In ancient times, upon completion or graduation, students were identified as sons and daughters of light, child of light, children of light or children of the sun. Why do you think they were given those names? What did they aspire to achieve after 42 years of learning?

As mentioned above, in Kemet the sun symbolized knowledge. Even today when a person is considered smart, we often say that he or she is "very bright." You might also notice that in various types of written or electronic media, when a character gets an idea we often see a light bulb shining over the character's head. You have probably seen it while watching a cartoon show on television or while reading your favorite comic book.

How did Kemetians view education? How did they teach children about the world and about their place in the world? What did they study?

Africans developed the most complex system of education to be found in early recorded history. Evidence of this educational system can be found in paintings, monuments, architecture, and technology and, above all, in the Medu Netcher (hieroglyphic) writings. It is also found in many of their stories, rituals, and songs which were passed down from one generation to the next.

Ancient Kemet was a high tech society that required thousands of educated people. The first step in the educational process (general education) was training as a scribe, which was considered to be a very high and honorable position in Kemetian society. The scribe school was the first step toward obtaining a sacred or secular position. Scribes began training by copying Medu Netcher. The subjects they copied were serious ones as opposed to nursery rhymes or beginner's alphabets. They were introduced to complex material at the beginning of their training. Initially, they may not have understood everything they copied but eventually they understood many of the greatest historical and spiritual teaching in the history of mankind.

Ancient Kemetians lived close to nature and the educational process of the people was greatly influenced by their environment. They made observations of natural processes that had taken place for over thousands of years. In the Nile Valley, as in other parts of the world, nature has a process of birth, growth, aging, death, decay, and rebirth. In their observation of this process, Kemetian people followed the laws of nature. The Nile Valley education system included the observation of the stars

and planets of the solar system. **Astronomy** was developed by Africans to measure scientific data about the movement of the planets and the sun.

The ultimate aim of education in Kemet was for a person to "become one with God" or to develop God-like qualities. In order to do this, the student needed to develop **character** (the specific thoughts, manners, actions and behaviors of a person) and a **moral compass** (having qualities such as honesty, courage, truthfulness and doing the right thing even when no one is watching). How might students develop character? Which characteristics were most important for them to develop?

To aid students in developing the desired character, they used **a list of virtues**. Students were taught that every *action* in which you engage is a direct result of your *thoughts*. Maintaining *correct thoughts* would continue to produce *desired results*. It is from these higher ideals that they were allowed to realize their *reason for being* and to understand their *mission* in life. Once they identified their mission, the student would be empowered with deep insight, and a call to *spiritual order* that equipped them with the courage necessary to accomplish their mission. A life of virtue was a condition required by those who were allowed to enter the Kemetian (Egyptian) institutions of higher learning. All students were expected to practice and demonstrate the following virtues as a part of their educational system:

1. **Control of Thought**
2. **Control of Action**
3. **Steadfastness of Purpose**
4. **Identify With Higher Ideals**
5. **Evidence of a Mission**
6. **Evidence of a Call to Spiritual Order**
7. **Freedom From Resentment (Courage)**
8. **Confidence in the Power of the Master (Teacher)**
9. **Confidence in One's Own Learning Abilities**
10. **Preparedness for Initiation**

Some of the specific educational goals of study were:
1. Unity of the person, unity of the family and community, and unity with nature
2. The development of social responsibility.
3. The development of character.
4. The development of spiritual power.

In Kemet's educational system, there was not a big focus on grades or test scores of students. More attention was given to the student's character as a reason for failure or success in school. The learning process included time for stories, examination of signs and symbols, the use of proverbs, and the use of songs and dance. These were all combined to teach values and a harmonious view of the world. Teachers modeled the behavior they wanted their students to learn.

Serious education began by putting the **initiate** (beginner) on the path of observation to learn the laws of matter (materials). Some of the most important parts of the educational process were conducted in secret and passed on orally to the prepared students, who were called "initiates". The initiate was assigned to a master craftsman as an apprentice. During this **apprenticeship**, initiates had to prove that they could use good judgment and that they were responsible. The path to the development of godlike qualities was through the development of virtue, and virtue could only be achieved through special study and effort under the guidance and examples of Master Teachers.

Ultimately, Kemetians sought **Ma'at,** an African-centered concept based on the belief of unchanging laws that govern the universe. According to Dr. C. Tsehloane Keto in his book, *The African Centered Perspective of History*, "Ma'at is the essence of a social justice as practiced by the Ancient Africans of the Nile." Everyone was expected to follow the code of ethics established according to Ma'at, including the Nsw (Queens) and Nswt (Kings/Pharaohs). This included "laws" that guided them in how to care for their body and respect the laws of nature: the earth, the waterways, the air and the ozone. They understood the importance of maintaining balance in nature.

Symbol of Ma'at

Photos by Sya - JNK, CC 2016 – British Museum

The Ma'at symbol was often carved on coffins and within the burial chambers as shown by the photos above.

Ma'at represented the following 7 virtues, or principles:

1. truth
2. justice
3. righteousness
4. harmony

5. balance
6. reciprocity
7. order

Chapter 11: Mdw Ntr (Medu Netcher)

You will discover:

1. Why Ancient Kemites(Egyptians) named their language Mdw Ntr
2. How both letters and pictures were used in the Kemetic "alphabet"
3. Where proof may be found that Mdw Ntr existed as the earliest form of written expression.

Important words to know:

Mdw Ntr	inscription	Scribe
metaphor	Medu Netcher	Kemwer
abolish	theory	Mason
vocal symbols	visual representation	hieroglyphs

Sacred Language and Script

Do you know of any languages that uses pictures and letters? Can you name any languages that can be read left to right and right to left? One such language, called **Mdw Ntr**, was developed hundreds of thousands of years ago in Africa. Mdw Ntr (pronounced **Medu Netcher**) is the oldest written language dating back to 3300 B.C.E. and before. To the Kemetians, Mdw Ntr meant "the words of God or Divine speech". When the Greeks invaded Kemet in 332 B.C.E. they changed the name of the language to hieroglyphs (meaning sacred **inscription**). Language helps us to express our ideas. How people define themselves comes from how they name and describe their language. Mdw Ntr was both a language and a script for the Ancient Kemetians. As a language it had an organized structure of vocal symbols by which people communicated. As a script it was a visual representation of all the sounds of the language and took the form of written signs and symbols.

In Kemet, there was no separation between the attributes of humans, the creator and nature. Although the birds, bees, fish in the sea and the two legged and four legged creatures are physically different, they were all considered to be a part of the unity and order needed to have a balanced organized universe. This inclusive, harmonious view of the world showed up in the writing - Medu Netcher- of Kemet. The love and respect for all of life, including humans, animals, plants, minerals and aquatic beings are shown in more than eight hundred symbols created in the Mdw Ntr (Medu Netcher) language. Mdw Ntr is seen everywhere, such as monuments, temples, coffins, and pyramids among other places. The word for writing was the same word used for painting and drawing. People

who were trained to write the script (Medu Netcher) were called **scribes**. Remember, a scribe's job was to make sure that the culture and history of Kemet were preserved and never forgotten.

> **Medu Netcher is considered to be the first "alphabet chart" in history.**

The Medu Netcher language was abolished in 550 A.D. and people were penalized if they were caught writing or reading it. During the same time, the Philae Temple which contained many of the artifacts was closed. It was the last temple to Auset and it was located in the city of Philae.

Here are some words Kemites used to describe themselves and their country:

Word	Meaning
Kemet (Kmt)	Land (nation) of the Blacks
KM	Black
Kemwer	Egyptian person, place, thing ("to be black, great")

Photo by Sya – JNK, CC 2016 British Museum

Spirit Door of Ptahshepses, high priest of Ptah in Kemet's capital in Memphis.

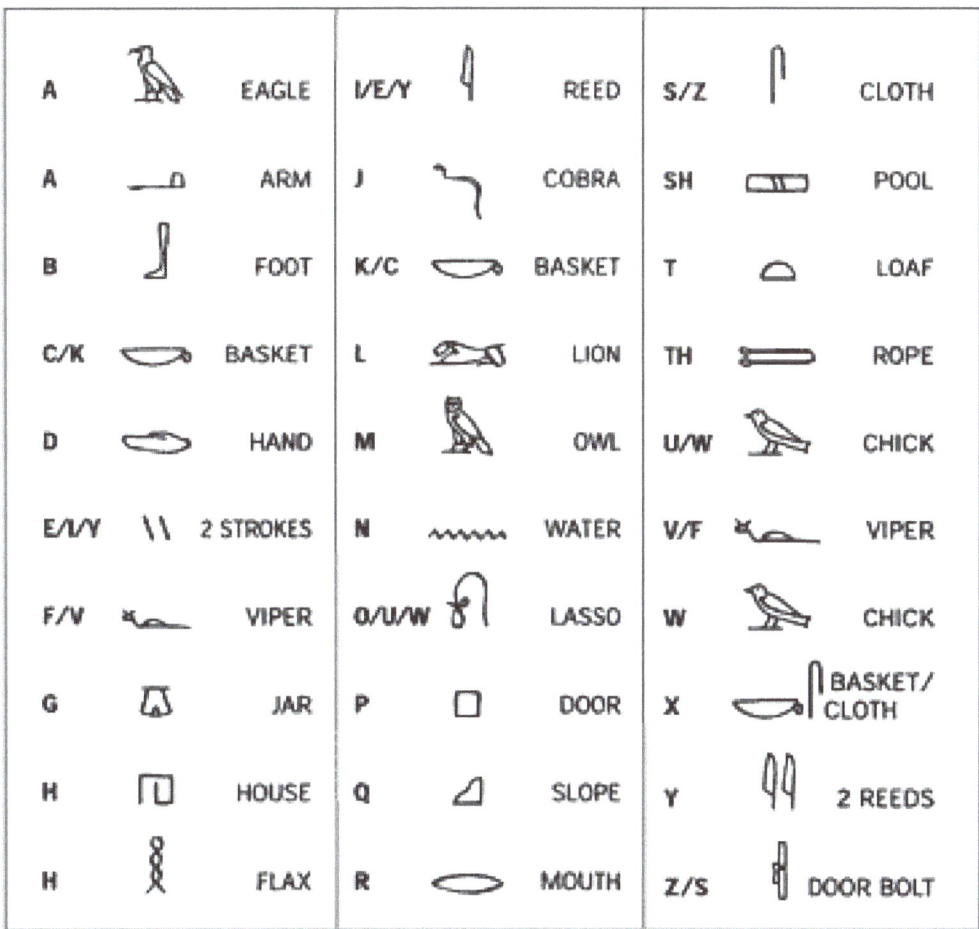

Illustration of the 30 Basic of Mdw Ntr (Medu Netcher) – Hieroglyphic Symbols

Technology allows us to stay connected to this ancient language today.

Numbers in Mdw Ntr (Hieroglyphics)

Have you ever thought about who invented a method of counting, or a number system? How do you know to write "1" for one item or 10 for ten items? The Ancient Kemetians invented a system so they would be able to count. They wrote a vertical stroke for one (Example: | = 1) and continued to add a stroke for each additional one (Example: || = 2 and ||||||| = 7). Can you imagine how many strokes it would take if they wrote individual strokes to count 25, 100 or 500? Instead of writing a single stroke for every number, they used symbols to represent a larger number. For example, they used a symbol like this (∩) to represent the number 10. Below, you can see how they combined symbols and strokes to increase the total number.

∩| = 1   ∩||||| = 15   ∩||||||||| = 19   ⋒ = 20   ⋒||||| = 25   ⋒⋒ = 30

Below are other symbols in Kemet's number system and their meaning:

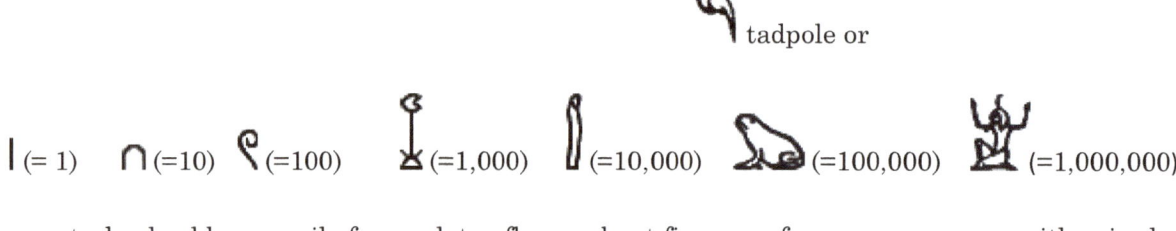

| (= 1)   ∩ (=10)   ℓ (=100)   (=1,000)   (=10,000)   (=100,000) tadpole or frog   (=1,000,000)

one stroke   heel bone   coil of rope   lotus flower   bent finger   frog   man with raised hands

Can you calculate the total number represented on the inscription above?

Part Seven

Kemetic Symbolism and Metaphors

Chapter 12: Signs of the Time in Kemet

Symbols were a very important part of the language and life in Kemet. They used symbols from nature to express ideas, concepts and values that aligned with principles of Ma'at. One such symbol is the sun. However, people in Kemet did not worship the sun, stars or animals; rather, they used them as symbolic expressions of the divine aspect of God.

On the following pages, you will see some symbols that are commonly associated with Kemet and their meaning.

Ankh – Symbol of Life

It represents the unification of feminine and masculine forces in the universe and the creation of new life.

Ma'at – Symbol of truth, justice, balance, reciprocity, and harmony.

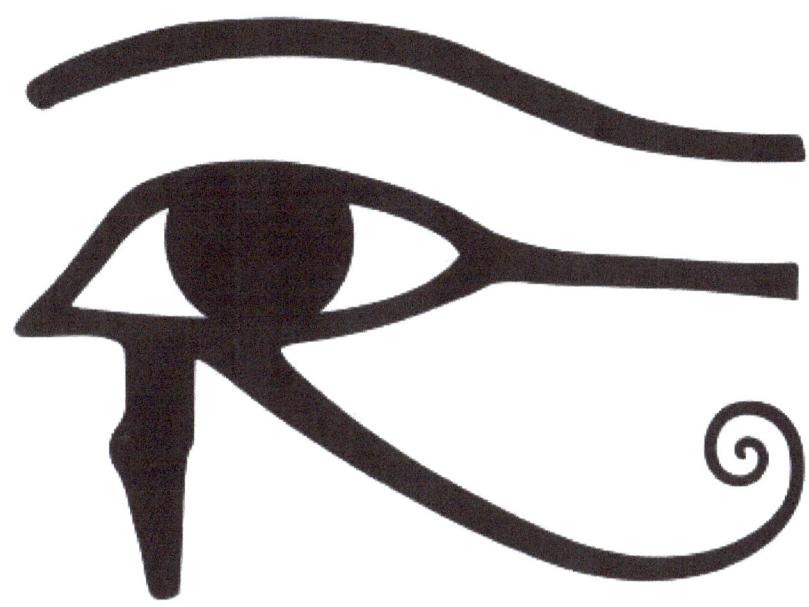

Eye of Horus (Heru) – Symbol of light in the heavens: the Sun and the Moon.

Kheper (Dung Beetle) – Symbol of transformation and the process of resurrection, or rebirth.

Fun Fact:

The Pyramid of Unas includes inscriptions that are known as "Pyramid Text". It is one of many papyrus scrolls and writings that were found in tombs and subsequently included in a publication called, "Book of the Dead". The Ancient Egyptians called this book, Reu nu Prt em hru (The Chapters of Coming Forth by Day). **It is the oldest known book of scriptures in the world.**

Review Questions

Read the directions and answer the questions below.

1. Explain why Kemetians called their language Mdw Ntr?

2. Fill in the blank spaces:

   Students were called _____ after they finished ____ years of education in Kemet.

3. When was Medu Netcher abolished?

4. Fill in the blank spaces:

   When the _____ invaded Kemet in ____, they changed the name of the language from Medu Netcher to _____.

5. Based on the information provided in your textbook, why do you think that Mdw Ntr was **abolished**. Support your **theory** (what you think is true) with statements from the text or any other supporting resources.

6. Draw a design or logo that you would like to wear on a T-shirt that would tell people something about you or something important to you.

7. Using the Kemetic number system chart, write the Kemetic expression (symbol) for:

   30_____   200_____

   50_____   100,001_____

Summary

Three thousand years of uninterrupted development along the Nile Valley positioned Africans to have a major influence on the world that still continues to this day. There is a lot of evidence and data that show historical and present connections between Kemet, the continent of Africa and other parts of the world. This connection is sometimes referred to as a **cultural unity** because of the common ideas, languages and history people share although they live in different regions. In the next volume of this series, we will examine some of the additional aspects of cultural unity that continues to demonstrate how we are all connected: past, present and future.

SYA (knowledge)

"Human history was born on the African continent which makes Africa the wellspring from which all of the world's history flows. Africa was the birthplace of art and music; the first writing, agriculture and systems of laws. Africa gave us the blue print for civilization itself. These records speak to us across millennia as profound refutations of the claim that Africans lacked a history before Europeans arrived."

Henry Louis Gates, Jr.

A people without the knowledge of their past history, origin and culture is like a tree without roots. - Marcus Garvey

Glossary

A. D. – abbreviation for "Anno Domini", a Latin phrase that means "in the year of our Lord". It refers to the year Christ was born. (Example: 300 A.D. refers to the time 300 years after the birth of Christ)

B. C. – abbreviation for "before Christ". Both A.D. and B.C. are used to label or number years used with the Julian and Gregorian calendars. Example: 300 B.C. refers to the time 300 years before the before Christ.)

abolish – a-bol-ish: To do away with; put an end to, annul. To destroy completely.

Abu Simbel – Site of two temples created by Ramesses II about 1250 BCE; located in northern Nubia.

agriculture - ag·ri·cul·ture: the science or practice of farming, including preparing the soil (dirt) for growing crops (vegetables and fruit) and caring for animals that provide food, wool and other products.

Alkebu-lan: The ancient name the indigenous people (Moors and Ethiopians) called their continent before the Greeks and Romans changed it to "Africa".

ankh - ankh: the Egyptian symbol of eternal life.

antiseptic – an-ti-sep-tic: Capable of preventing infection by inhibiting (stopping) the growth of infectious agents.

apprenticeship ap-pren-tice: A person who is a beginner learning a trade or occupation and usually is a member of a labor union for the trade that he or she is learning, such as a plumber or electrician.

Anthropologist- an-thro-po-lo-gist: A scientist who studies the origin, behavior and physical, social and cultural development of humans.

Archaeologist - ar·chae·ol·o·gy or ar·che·ol·o·gy (är′kē-ŏl′ə-jē): the scientific study of material remains (example: artifacts, fossil relics, monuments) of past human life and activities. A study of the remains of the culture of a people.

artifact - ar·ti·fact also ar·te·fact (är′tə-făkt′): an object made by a human being that has cultural or historical interest

character-char-ac-ter (kăr′ək-tər): Moral strength; integrity. A person considered as having a specific quality or attribute.

civilization – civ-i-li-za-tion (sĭv′ə-lĭ-zā′shən): An advanced state of intellectual, cultural, and material development in human society, marked by progress in the arts and sciences, extensive use of record-keeping, including writing, and the appearance of complex political and social institutions

contradicton – con-tra-dic-tion (kon-trə-dik-shən): An inconsistency or discrepancy

colonization- col-o-ni-za-tion (kŏl′ə-nĭ-zā′shən) : The act or process of establishing new colonies.

coregent- co-re-gent (kəʊˈriːdʒənt):a joint regent, as ruler or governor, such as in government, politics and diplomacy

cultural unity- cul-tu-ral (kul-chər-əl) u-ni-ty (yo͞o-ni-te): The things a group of people has in common that binds them together, such as traditions, language, art, crafts and many other things.

cultivate – cul-ti-vate (kŭl′tə-vāt′):to till and prepare land or soil for the growth of crops

deity - de·i·ty (dē′ĭ-tē, dā′-) : a god or goddess; a state of being divine

diplomat- di·plo·mat (dĭp′lə-măt′): One who has been appointed, such as an ambassador, to represent a country in its relations with other governments.

diplomacy - di·plo·ma·cy (dĭ-plō′mə-sē) the skill of managing international relations with a country's representative

domesticate-do·mes·ti·cate (də-mes-ti-kat): To train or adapt an animal or plant to live in a human environment and be of use to humans. To introduce an animal or plant to another region.

dynasty - dy·nas·ty (di-nə-stē): A period of rulership by one or more families.

economy - e·con·o·my (ĭ-kŏn′ə-mē): the wealth and resources of a country or region, especially the production and consumption of goods and services

Egyptologist - E·gyp·tol·o·gist (ē′jĭp-tŏl′ə jēst)): a person who studies ancient Egyptian history, culture, language, literature religion, architecture and art, primarily focusing on the period after the 25th dynasty and foreign invasion.

Empress -

em·press (ĕm′prĭs): The woman ruler of an empire. The wife or widow of an emperor.

People in Kemet called an empress, or queen, "**hemtnesew**".

equator – e·qua·tor (e-kwa-tər): The imaginary circle around the earth's surface that divides the earth into the Northern and Southern Hemispheres.

erect - e·rect (ĭ-rĕkt′): to construct, or build (a building, statue, pyramid, wall or any other upright structure

excavation-ex·ca·va·tion (ek-skə-va-shən): the act of digging a hole, such as an archaeological site

fossil- fos-sil (fŏs′əl): A trace of an organism of a past geologic age, such as a skeleton or leaf imprint, which has been preserved in the Earth's crust.

Herodotus – He·ro·do·tus: Earliest Greek historian who visited Kemet and documented his travels in a book called *History*.

hieroglyphics – hi·er·gly·phics (hī′ər-ə-glĭf′ĭks): System of writing created in Ancient Kemet (Egypt) using pictures, or symbols, to represent meaning or sounds or a combination of meaning and sound.

Initiates- i-mi-ti-ates (ĭ-nĭsh′ē-āt′) : One who has been introduced to or obtained some knowledge in a particular field.

hominoid- hom-i-noid (hŏm′ə-noid′) : A primate of a group that includes humans, their fossil ancestors, and the anthropoid apes.

inscription - in·scrip·tion (ĭn-skrĭp′shən): A marking, such as the wording on a coin medal, monument or seal.

instrumental - in·stru·men·tal (ĭn′strə-mĕn′tl): serving as an important means in pursuing or contributing to something (example: He was instrumental in find the key that solved the mystery

invade - in·vade (in-vad): to enter a country by force

irrigate- ir-ri-gate: To supply (land or crops) with water by means of canals, pipes, ditches or streams.

Kemet - Name of the Northeast African nation now called Egypt. It means "Land of the Blacks"

Kemetologist - ke·me·tol·o·gist (ke-me- tol-ə jis) Term coined by Asa Hilliard, a historian who was dedicated to the study of Egypt during the time period in which Nile Valley Civilization existed and was called Kemet [1st – 25th Dynasties])

Kush – Nubian name of a kingdom which was used by the Egyptians and first noted in an inscription about 1,900 B.C.

MAAFA- term created by Marimba Ani to describe the African holocaust.

matriarchal - (ma-tre-är-kəl): A highly respected woman who is a mother and who rules a family.

Medu Netcher – Picture-writing of Ancient Kemet which originated in the Upper Nile Valley. Derived from "Medu (writing) "Netcher" (God) known as the "writing of God".

Meroe -Royal residence of Kush during the Meroitic Period, about 270 BCE to 350ACE

Metaphor- met-a-phor (mĕt′ə-fôr′, -fər): A figure of speech in which a word or phrase is used to describe an object or action to show, or imply, a similarity.

moral compass- mo-ral com-pass: That which serves or guides a person's knowledge, sense or intuition of correct virtues, morals or ethics.

mummify – mum-mi-fy (mŭm′ə-fī′): to make into a mummy by embalming and drying.

mural- mu-ral (myoor′əl): A very large image, such as a painting, applied directly to a wall or ceiling

Napata – Northern capital and chief religious center of the kingdom of Kush.

Nubia – Ancient country originally called Kush located to the North of the Nile Valley near Aswan. The culture developed in Nubia heavily influenced the civilization later established in Kemet.

obelisk - (Kemites refer to these as "tekhenu")- A monument of Ancient Egyptian first built in Ancient Egypt made of a tall stone and pyramid shape on top.

papyrus – Plant which grew along the Nile River that was used to make paper. The paper was used to create boats, baskets, sleeping mats, shoes and scrolls (sheets of paper) that were glued together to create books.

peace treaty: A written agreement between two states or soveriegns.

Pharaoh -Phar·aoh or phar·aoh (fâr′ō, fā′rō): Greek term for a king of ancient Egypt. a ruler in Ancient Egypt. Kemet people referred to a male leader (pharaoh) as **Per ah**.

philosopher-phi-lo-so-pher (fĭ-lŏs′ə-fər): A person who offers views or theories on profound questions in ethics, logic, metaphysics and other related fields ; a person who is well versed in their understanding of philosophy

preservation - pre·serve (prĭ-zûrv′): To keep from injury, peril, or harm; protect. to make something last

pyramid -pyr·a·mid (pĭr′ə-mĭd): Royalty tomb in use in Kemet from the Third Dynasty to the 17th Dynasty. Originally called " Mir" in Ancient Kemet)

quarry-quar-ry kwôr-re): An open excavation or pit from which stones are obtained by digging, cutting or blasting.

reed : Various tall perennial grasses having hollow stems and large plume like panicles that grows in wetlands, such as the papyrus.

reign-(rān): Period during which a monarch (leader of state or country) rules or exercises sovereign power

restoration- res-to-ra-tion (res-tə-ra-shən): the replacement or giving back of something lost, damaged, stolen; the act of replacing or reconstructing something
sage- (sāj): One recognized for experience, judgment and wisdom
scribe-(skrīb): People who were trained to write the script (Medu Netcher). A scribe's job was to document the culture and history of Kemet to make sure it was preserved.
social responsibility: An ethical theory that suggest all organizations and individuals have an oblilgation to act and make decisions that benefits society; to maintain balance between the economy and the ecosystem.
solar system- comprises the sun and its planetary systems of eight planets, their moons and other non-stellar objects. It was formed 4.6 billion years ago.
sustain-sus-tain (sə-stan): To keep in existence, maintain or continue something
scroll- (skrol): A roll, such as a parchment or papyrus, used especially for writing a document. An ancient book or volume written on a roll of paper.
theory-the-o-ry (the-ə-re): An assumption based on limited information or knowledge; A set of statements devised to explain a group of facts, especially one that has been repeatedly tested or widely used to make predictions.
vizier- vi-zier (vĭ-zîr', vĭz'yər): A high government official.
virtue- vir-tue (vûr'chōō) : High excellenee and righteousness; goodness
workforce-(wûrk-fôrs): The workers employed in a specific nation, company, industry or project.

Bibliography

SOURCES:

1. Angelou, Dr. Maya *Wouldn't Take Nothing for my Journey Now*. 1993
2. Bauval, Robert. *Imhotep the African: Architect of the Cosmos*.
3. Ben-Jochannan, Yosef A.A. *Black Man of the Nile and His Family*. 1989
4. Browder, Anthony T. *Nile Valley Contributions to Civilization*. Washington, D.C.: Institute of Karmic Guidance, 1992.
5. Browder, Anthony T. *Egypt on the Potomac* Washington, DC: Institute of Karmic Guidance
6. Browder, Anthony T. *From the Browder File* Washington, DC: Institute of Karmic Guidance
7. Finch III, Charles S. *The African Origins of Medicine, Sciences, Math & Religion*.
8. Harkless, Necia Desiree. Nubian Pharaohs and Meroitic Kings: The Kingdom of Kush; 2006
9. Heinrichs, Ann. *The Nile*. 2009
10. Hobbs, Joseph J. *Modern World Nations: Egypt*. 2007
11. Hunter, Havelin, Adams III, "*African and African-American Contributions to Science & Technology*, "African-American Baseline Essays, Portland, OR 1987, p. S41
12. Keto, C. Tsehloane, *The African Centered Perspective on History*
13. Klein, Christopher. *Discovery of Oldest Human Fossil fills Evolutionary Gap*; 2015
14. Williams, Chancellor. *The Destruction of Black Civilization: Great Issues of Race from 4500 B.C. to 2000 A.D.* 1987
15. Sertima, Dr. Ivan Van. *Black Women in Antiquity*. Revised Edition, 1984
16. Robinson, Calvin; Battle, Redman; Robinson, Edward W. *The Journey of the Songhai People*. 1st Edition, 1987
17. Brian Villmoare, William H. Kimbel, Chalachew Seyoum, Christopher J. Campisano, Erin DiMaggio, John Rowan; Science Journal; *Early Homo at 2.8 Ma from Ledi-Geraru Afar, Ethiopia*. 04 March 2015; aaa1343 DOI:10.1126/science.aaa1343

WEBSITES:

1. http://www.touregypt.net/19dyn02.htm   Accessed December 2015
2. https://www.youtube.com/watch?feature=player_embedded&v=1yK3EdnC9Vs. Accessed December 2015
3. https://www.youtube.com/watch?v=Oz8E96OI_Eg. Accessed December 2015
4. Rocknewmanshow.net/?p=1218
5. http://meduneter.com/ (From Kemet to DC, 2015)
6. https://www.saamr.org
7. http://www.houseoflifeabydos.com
8. https://zethio.files.wordpress.com/2014/04/the-timeline-of-african-american-history.pdf. Accessed January 2016
9. http://medu.ipetisut.com/ Accessed February 2016
10. http://www.touregypt.net/egypt-info/magazine-mag05012001-magf4.htm#ixzz4FvO00Qdg
11. Hidden Black History
12. https://www.mathstat.slu.edu
13. https://anthropology.msu.edu
14. American Heritage® Dictionary of the English Language, Fifth Edition. (2011). Retrieved September 15 2016 from http://www.thefreedictionary.com/

15. Collins English Dictionary – Complete and Unabridged, 12th Edition 2014 © HarperCollins Publishers 1991, 1994, 1998, 2000, 2003, 2006, 2007, 2009, 2011, 2014
16. https://www.history.com/news/discovery-of-oldest-human-fossil-fills-evolutionary-gap Accessed February 2018
17. wikipedia commons. (n.d.). Imhotep louvre. Retrieved from https://commons.wikimedia.org/wiki/File:Imhotep-Louvre.jpg

ILLUSTRATION CREDITS

1. Illustration, King Tut – Curt Cunningham, Artist 2016
2. Illustration, Kemetian students, L. Camper, 2016
3. Illustration, Eye of Horus, Jeff Dahl/Wikimedia Commons
4. Free Images - Free Stock Photos. Accessed February 07, 2016. http://www.freeimages.co.uk/.
   Free Photo: Children, Sudan, Smiling, Aid. Accessed February 07, 2016.
5. "Home - Creative Commons." Creative Commons. Accessed February 07, 2016. https://creativecommons.org/.
6. Map of Nile Valley Accessed July 13, 2016
7. Illustration: Continent of Africa, The True Size of Africa: A Small Contribution in the Fight Against Rampant Immappancy; Kai Krause

www.ingramcontent.com/pod-product-compliance
Lightning Source LLC
Chambersburg PA
CBHW051347110526
44591CB00025B/2935